Kai Lian

Rituals of Unity
Study of Li in Confucian Thought

Copyright
Original Title: *Rituais da Unidade*
Copyright © 2024 by Luiz Antonio dos Santos
All rights reserved to Booklas.com

This book is a philosophical and cultural work exploring Confucian thought and its applications in the contemporary world. Based on in-depth studies, historical references, and cultural analyses, its content aims to provide transformative reflection. This publication is intended for study, personal development, and intellectual enrichment and is not a substitute for professional, therapeutic, or academic advice.

Production Team
Translation and Adaptation: Amanda Taylor
Editor: Luiz Antonio dos Santos
Philosophical and Cultural Consultancy: Jian Wong, Mei Chen, Sakura Ishikawa
Text Review: Margaret Klein, Hana Saito
Graphic Design and Layout: Lisa Bennett
Cover Design: Studio Booklas / Gabriel Fonseca

Publication and Identification
Rituals of Unity / By Kai Lian
Booklas, 2024
Categories: Philosophy. History. Chinese Culture. Personal Development.
I. Lian, Kai. II. Bennett, Lisa. III. Title.
DDC: 181.112 - CDU: 181.1

All Rights Reserved
Booklas Publishing
962 José Delalíbera Street
86.183-550 – Cambé – PR – Brazil
E-mail: suporte@booklas.com
Website: www.booklas.com

Summary

Prologue 5
Chapter 1 Ancient Origins 8
Chapter 2 The Eternal Master 12
Chapter 3 Foundational Thought 16
Chapter 4 Social Context 20
Chapter 5 Cultural Influences 24
Chapter 6 Classical Texts 28
Chapter 7 The Confucian School 32
Chapter 8 The Philosophical Tradition 36
Chapter 9 Essential Virtue 40
Chapter 10 True Humanity 44
Chapter 11 Natural Justice 49
Chapter 12 Sacred Rituals 54
Chapter 13 Practical Wisdom 58
Chapter 14 Mutual Trust 62
Chapter 15 Universal Harmony 66
Chapter 16 Natural Order 70
Chapter 17 Social Hierarchy 74
Chapter 18 Filial Piety 78
Chapter 19 Family Bonds 82
Chapter 20 Governmental Relationships 86
Chapter 21 Virtuous Friendship 91
Chapter 22 Mutual Respect 95
Chapter 23 Social Responsibility 99
Chapter 24 Familial Harmony 103

Chapter 25 Personal Cultivation 107
Chapter 26 Lifelong Learning 112
Chapter 27 Moral Education 116
Chapter 28 Practical Knowledge 121
Chapter 29 Intellectual Development 125
Chapter 30 Integral Formation 129
Chapter 31 Moral Example 133
Chapter 32 Applied Wisdom 137
Chapter 33 Virtuous Politics 142
Chapter 34 Moral Leadership 146
Chapter 35 Social Order 150
Chapter 36 Public Administration 154
Chapter 37 The Common Good 159
Chapter 38 Governmental Justice 164
Chapter 39 Political Harmony 168
Chapter 40 Social Reform 172
Chapter 41 Practical Rituals 176
Chapter 42 Daily Conduct 180
Chapter 43 Social Etiquette 184
Chapter 44 Moral Practice 188
Chapter 45 Spiritual Cultivation 193
Chapter 46 Personal Harmony 197
Chapter 47 Individual Discipline 202
Chapter 48 Everyday Wisdom 207
Chapter 49 Global Influence 211
Chapter 50 Modernity and Confucianism 216
Chapter 51 Cultural Dialogue 221

Chapter 52 Contemporary Challenges 226
Chapter 53 Eternal Legacy 231
Epilogue 235

Prologue

The chaos that shapes and distorts history, the conflicts that corrode the collective soul of a civilization, and the truths that remain hidden beneath the veil of time... This is the fertile ground where transformative ideas take root. You are about to embark on a unique journey that transcends the boundaries of common understanding and invites the discovery of an eternal foundation of harmony.

The book you hold in your hands is not merely a work about a tumultuous period in ancient China. It is a mirror reflecting universal questions, crossing the barriers of time and space. Each page carries the weight of centuries of wisdom, condensed into concepts that challenge norms and resonate with the deepest fibers of your being. This is not a cold academic text; it is an invitation to transcendence, an opportunity to reconnect with values that can transform lives, societies, and the very essence of what it means to be human.

Imagine living in a time when every action was a ritual, and every ritual was a link to the cosmos. In this context, political disorder and moral decay were not merely social challenges but cries of a humanity disconnected from what made it whole. It was in this setting that a man, Confucius, and a philosophy, Confucianism, emerged as responses to an existential void. Yet, do not think Confucianism belongs solely to the past. It echoes in modernity, pointing the way forward in a world equally chaotic and fragmented.

This book is more than a historical or philosophical narrative; it is a guide to reconstructing a lost balance. Confucius's ideas are not confined to an era or a people; they engage with the aspirations of those seeking harmony amidst modern chaos. It is for you, who wish to understand the power of rituals as vehicles for transformation, the importance of virtue as a unifying force, and the relevance of ethical leadership in times of crisis.

As you dive into the pages that follow, you will find lessons that transcend dogma. The ideas presented here do not impose; they illuminate. What is justice if not a reflection of inner harmony? What are rituals if not tools to align the human with the transcendent? And virtue, so often explored and yet forgotten— what can it be but the path that links individual morality to collective well-being?

If you feel something essential is missing in the way the world operates, this book offers answers. It does not promise easy or quick solutions. On the contrary, it demands that you face the complexities of existence and morality with courage and depth. But it offers something rare: an opportunity to see beyond the visible, to question the foundations of what you consider true, and to transform that quest into a living practice.

There is no coincidence in the fact that you are here, now, holding this book. There is a reason it has found its way to you, and there is a quiet calling within its pages, waiting to be answered. Will you accept the challenge? The pages are open, and the journey begins.

Translated and Adapted from the Original Work Rituais da Unidade

By Amanda Taylor

Chapter 1
Ancient Origins

The story begins amidst the fragmented landscapes of ancient China, a world defined by its deep connections to the earth and sky, yet torn apart by relentless conflict. The era of the Warring States (475-221 BCE) was a crucible of disarray and innovation. With the collapse of the Zhou dynasty's once-centralized authority, smaller states clashed in pursuit of dominance, scattering the ideals of harmony and order like leaves in a gale.

It was a time when the bonds of kinship and tradition were strained under the weight of warfare, economic upheaval, and shifting alliances. The decentralized political structure left vast swaths of land to the mercy of warlords, each vying to expand their dominion. Towns crumbled, borders shifted, and the people longed for stability in the midst of chaos. Yet, within this fragmentation, a fertile ground was prepared for the emergence of radical thought.

Rituals and social structures, once revered as the backbone of civilization, were slowly losing their grip. The veneration of ancestors persisted, a flickering flame against the encroaching darkness, while the celestial mandate—Tian—still provided hope that order could be restored. It was not merely chaos but an opportunity for transformation, a dawn awaiting its herald. This was the stage upon which Confucius, and the ideas that would bear his name, would one day tread.

But before Confucius could carve his legacy, the forces shaping his philosophy had already begun their inexorable work. The ideals of kinship, responsibility, and moral order had long been embedded within Chinese society, reinforced by millennia of collective practice. Yet, these ideals were under siege by the harsh realities of the era. The rise of powerful regional lords, whose focus was conquest rather than compassion, forced communities into survival mode, often at the expense of communal harmony.

Even so, the past offered a blueprint for resilience. The Xia, Shang, and early Zhou dynasties had set the foundation for a worldview that cherished balance and reciprocity. The "Mandate of Heaven," a concept introduced during the Zhou era, linked morality with cosmic order, suggesting that just rule was intertwined with the divine. Yet, this idea faced a critical test as rulers faltered and their kingdoms fractured. The desperate search for a guiding philosophy intensified.

Philosophical schools of thought emerged from the debris, each claiming to hold the key to salvation. Legalists proposed a strict, authoritarian structure of rewards and punishments, while Daoists looked to the natural flow of the cosmos, urging withdrawal from worldly concerns. Yet, the Confucian vision, though nascent and unformed, was unique in its conviction: that humanity could transcend its suffering not through retreat or domination, but through the restoration of moral integrity and communal bonds.

This conviction, however, was not born in isolation. Long before Confucius's birth, the cultural traditions of ancestral worship, the ritualistic honoring of Tian, and the celebration of communal rites had shaped the collective psyche. These practices, though diminished by the strife of the Warring States, endured as living symbols of the harmony that was possible when humanity aligned itself with natural and moral laws.

Confucius would later draw upon these cultural undercurrents, breathing new life into ancient wisdom. He recognized that the struggles of his time were not merely material but spiritual—a disconnection between humanity and its intrinsic moral compass. This disconnection was not inevitable, he believed, but the product of neglect and ignorance. What was needed was a new synthesis, a philosophy that could reconcile tradition with the pressing needs of the present.

The tension between continuity and change defined the intellectual landscape of the Warring States. Scholars and visionaries debated the nature of governance, virtue, and the very purpose of existence. Could a ruler succeed by embodying virtue alone, or were harsh laws required to maintain order? Were individuals inherently good, as some claimed, or driven by selfish desires? These questions reverberated through the corridors of power and the streets of crumbling cities.

Amidst these debates, the foundations of Confucian thought began to crystallize, though its founder had yet to take his first breath. It was a vision that sought to harmonize the personal and the political, to restore balance to a world teetering on the edge of ruin.

This vision was shaped not only by the chaos of the Warring States but by a collective yearning for a return to moral clarity. The Confucian answer was radical in its simplicity: the restoration of virtue, not through external force but through the cultivation of the self. This philosophy would later resonate with rulers and peasants alike, promising a path to harmony that began within the individual and extended outward to encompass families, communities, and entire nations.

The roots of Confucianism, however, were firmly planted in the soil of its time. It was not an abstract philosophy divorced from reality, but a response to the tangible suffering and disillusionment of the age. The moral decay witnessed during this period demanded a counterbalance, and Confucius's ideas emerged as both a critique of the present and a call to rediscover humanity's highest potential.

The echoes of the Warring States era would reverberate throughout Chinese history, shaping not only Confucian thought but the broader cultural and political landscape. It was a time of paradox, where destruction paved the way for renewal, and despair gave birth to hope.

Through this lens, the origins of Confucianism become not merely a historical curiosity but a testament to the resilience of human ideals. The chaos that surrounded its emergence was not a sign of failure but a necessary precursor to its eventual flourishing. It was in the crucible of suffering and uncertainty that the seeds of Confucius's vision were sown, seeds that would grow into a philosophy that transcended its time and place.

Thus, the ancient origins of Confucianism reveal a profound truth: that even amidst the darkest turmoil, the light of wisdom can emerge. It is a reminder that the search for harmony, though fraught with obstacles, is a journey worth undertaking—a journey that begins with understanding the roots of our shared humanity. This understanding, as Confucianism teaches, is the first step toward creating a world where virtue reigns and chaos subsides.

Chapter 2
The Eternal Master

The figure of Confucius rises not as a mythic hero born of legend but as a man deeply intertwined with the struggles and aspirations of his time. Born in the small state of Lu during the tumultuous sixth century BCE, he entered a world where the echoes of collapsing traditions reverberated through daily life. His early years, marked by both adversity and determination, foreshadowed the philosophical legacy he would leave behind—a legacy born not of conquest, but of wisdom.

Confucius, or Kong Qiu, was born in 551 BCE to a family of modest means, descending from a once-prominent lineage that had fallen into obscurity. His father, Shuliang He, had served as a military officer, a man of discipline and strength. Yet the family's fortunes dwindled after his death when Confucius was still a young boy. Raised by his mother, Yan Zhengzai, Confucius grew up in an environment where survival required ingenuity and perseverance.

From an early age, Confucius demonstrated an insatiable curiosity and a profound respect for learning. His childhood, though humble, was filled with the teachings of past generations. He absorbed the values of filial piety and reverence for tradition, traits that would later anchor his philosophy. Despite the economic challenges his family faced, he sought out knowledge wherever it could be found, viewing education not as a privilege but as a moral duty.

As he matured, Confucius's experiences in Lu exposed him to the stark disparities of his time. The state, once a beacon of Zhou dynasty culture, had descended into a microcosm of the broader chaos gripping China. Corruption festered within the ruling elite, and power struggles among noble families eroded the integrity of governance. Amid this disarray, Confucius began to envision a path to restore harmony, a vision that would consume his life's work.

In his youth, Confucius took on a variety of roles, including positions in minor administrative posts. These experiences provided him with firsthand insight into the complexities of governance and the failures of those who wielded power. He observed how greed, incompetence, and a lack of moral clarity undermined the social order, deepening the suffering of ordinary people. These observations became the foundation for his belief that virtuous leadership was the key to societal harmony.

His career as an educator blossomed during this period. Recognizing the transformative power of knowledge, Confucius began teaching students from diverse backgrounds, breaking with the aristocratic norms of his time. For him, education was a means to cultivate virtue, not merely to impart skills or knowledge. His teachings emphasized the interconnectedness of moral development, family stability, and political integrity.

Confucius's philosophy emerged not as a rigid doctrine but as a dynamic response to the challenges of his era. He emphasized the concept of Ren, often translated as humanity or benevolence, as the cornerstone of ethical conduct. For Confucius, Ren was not an abstract ideal but a lived reality—a practice of empathy, compassion, and respect that began with the self and radiated outward to encompass family, community, and the state.

Equally central to his teachings was the idea of Li, or ritual propriety. Confucius viewed rituals not merely as ceremonial acts but as expressions of deeper moral principles. Through rituals, individuals could cultivate discipline, humility, and a sense of belonging to the greater whole. In his view, rituals served as a bridge between the past and present, preserving tradition while fostering continuity in a rapidly changing world.

Confucius also championed Yi, or righteousness, as a guiding principle for decision-making. For him, Yi represented the ability to act with integrity, even when faced with difficult choices. It was not enough to follow rules or seek personal gain; true righteousness required aligning one's actions with a higher moral standard.

As his reputation grew, Confucius attracted a following of dedicated disciples. These students, drawn by his vision of a just and harmonious society, carried his teachings far beyond the borders of Lu. Together, they debated the virtues of leadership, the nature of justice, and the role of tradition in modern governance. Confucius's relationship with his disciples was more than that of a teacher and pupils—it was a shared quest for wisdom, a dialogue that sought to reconcile the ideals of the past with the realities of the present.

Despite his intellectual influence, Confucius faced significant challenges in his efforts to implement his ideas on a broader scale. He traveled extensively, offering his counsel to rulers across the fractured states of China. Yet many of these rulers, consumed by ambition and short-term gains, rejected his vision of moral governance. Confucius's unwavering commitment to virtue often placed him at odds with the pragmatic demands of political survival.

His journey was marked by moments of profound disappointment. Time and again, Confucius encountered resistance to his belief that ethical leadership could restore order. Yet these setbacks only deepened his resolve. He saw himself not as a failure but as a vessel for a truth that transcended his own lifetime. For Confucius, the pursuit of virtue was its own reward, a path that required patience and perseverance in the face of adversity.

Toward the later years of his life, Confucius returned to Lu, where he focused on compiling and refining the teachings that would become the foundation of Confucian thought. He dedicated himself to preserving the wisdom of the past, curating texts such as the Book of Songs, the Book of Rites, and the Spring and

Autumn Annals. These works, infused with his commentary and interpretation, became the pillars of a philosophical tradition that would endure for millennia.

Confucius's legacy was not fully realized during his lifetime. He died in 479 BCE, leaving behind a vision that his disciples and their successors would labor to preserve and expand. Yet even in death, Confucius's influence continued to grow. His teachings, initially overlooked by many, began to resonate more deeply as China grappled with the need for stability and moral clarity in the centuries that followed.

Confucius was, above all, a man who believed in the transformative power of virtue. His life exemplified the ideals he sought to instill in others: humility, perseverance, and an unwavering commitment to the common good. He was not a prophet or a saint but a teacher, a seeker of truth who understood that the path to harmony began with the cultivation of the self.

Through his life and work, Confucius became the eternal master—a figure whose teachings transcended time and space, offering a beacon of hope and wisdom for those who sought to navigate the complexities of human existence. His vision of a world guided by virtue remains as relevant today as it was in the turbulent era of the Warring States, a testament to the enduring power of moral clarity in the face of chaos.

Continue sequencialmente observe as diretrizes para as seguir. Continue em inglês.

Chapter 3
Foundational Thought

Confucius's philosophy was born from a deep understanding of humanity's potential and its flaws, a tapestry woven with moral ideals and practical wisdom. At its heart were concepts that transcended the political turmoil of his era, offering a vision for a harmonious society built upon individual virtue and collective responsibility. These foundational ideas—Ren (humanity), Li (ritual propriety), Yi (righteousness), and Tian (the moral mandate of Heaven)—formed a cohesive framework that continues to resonate across centuries.

Ren, the cornerstone of Confucian thought, radiates as an ideal of humanity in its most noble form. Often translated as benevolence or compassion, Ren represents the innate capacity for kindness that binds individuals to one another. For Confucius, this virtue was not reserved for saints or sages but was accessible to all who sought to cultivate it through reflection and action. Ren was not simply a feeling; it demanded practice, seen in acts of empathy, respect, and moral courage.

The essence of Ren was captured in Confucius's words: "Do not impose on others what you do not wish for yourself." This golden rule extended beyond personal relationships to encompass governance and leadership, insisting that those in positions of power act with the welfare of the people in mind. Ren, in this sense, was both a personal and social virtue, requiring individuals to consider the ripple effects of their actions on the broader community.

Li, often described as ritual propriety, was equally central to Confucius's vision. While rituals in the traditional sense might evoke images of formal ceremonies or sacred rites, Confucius expanded the concept to include the patterns of behavior that shape daily life. Li encompassed everything from family obligations and social etiquette to the governance of a state, serving as a structure that maintained order and harmony.

For Confucius, rituals were not mere formalities but expressions of deeper moral principles. Through Li, individuals learned to cultivate self-discipline and respect, reinforcing the bonds that held society together. A bow of courtesy, a gesture of gratitude, or the observance of ancestral rites were not trivial acts but reflections of an inner commitment to harmony and reverence. By practicing Li, individuals aligned themselves with the moral fabric of their communities and the cosmic order.

Yi, or righteousness, added another layer to this philosophical framework. Yi demanded that individuals act according to what was just and morally correct, even in the face of adversity. It was a virtue that resisted compromise, emphasizing integrity over expedience. Where Ren encouraged empathy and kindness, Yi served as the unwavering compass that guided individuals through ethical dilemmas.

For Confucius, the interplay between Yi and Ren was crucial. While Ren inspired compassion, Yi ensured that this compassion did not lead to indulgence or moral weakness. Together, they created a balance between understanding others and upholding the principles that sustain a just society. Yi was the force that allowed individuals to confront corruption and injustice, even at personal cost, embodying the courage to act rightly despite external pressures.

Underpinning these concepts was Tian, often translated as Heaven, but more accurately described as a moral and cosmic order. In the Confucian worldview, Tian represented an overarching principle of justice and harmony that governed both the natural and human realms. It was neither a deity nor an abstract force but an ethical mandate that required individuals and rulers to align themselves with its values.

The concept of the Mandate of Heaven, inherited from earlier Chinese thought, served as a cornerstone of Confucian philosophy. Tian granted legitimacy to rulers who governed with virtue and compassion, and it revoked that legitimacy when they acted with selfishness or tyranny. This principle held rulers accountable, suggesting that their authority was not absolute but conditional upon their moral conduct.

Through Tian, Confucius connected individual virtue to the broader order of the universe. He saw humanity's role as one of alignment with this cosmic order, suggesting that personal cultivation and ethical governance were essential to maintaining balance in both the earthly and celestial realms. This belief imbued his teachings with a sense of purpose that transcended the immediate concerns of politics and society.

Confucius also emphasized the importance of education as a vehicle for cultivating these virtues. For him, learning was not merely about acquiring knowledge but about shaping character and fostering a sense of moral responsibility. Education was the path through which individuals could achieve self-improvement, a process he referred to as self-cultivation.

Self-cultivation began with the recognition of one's shortcomings and the commitment to overcome them through reflection and disciplined practice. Confucius believed that anyone, regardless of their social status, could achieve moral excellence through education and effort. This democratization of virtue was revolutionary in an age when privilege often dictated opportunity.

Confucius's focus on education extended to his belief in the power of example. He taught that leaders, whether of families or nations, must embody the virtues they sought to instill in others. The moral authority of a ruler or teacher depended not on their position but on their character. "The virtuous person," Confucius declared, "is like the North Star, which remains in its place while all other stars turn toward it."

This emphasis on leading by example underscored the interconnectedness of Confucius's philosophy. Virtue was not an isolated pursuit but a force that radiated outward, influencing families, communities, and entire states. By cultivating their own character, individuals contributed to the collective well-being, creating a ripple effect that extended far beyond their immediate actions.

Confucius's foundational thought also highlighted the dynamic relationship between tradition and innovation. While he revered the wisdom of the past, particularly the Zhou dynasty's emphasis on moral governance and ritual, he adapted these principles to address the challenges of his time. He sought to preserve what was timeless while remaining responsive to the needs of a changing world.

This balance between continuity and adaptation became a hallmark of Confucian philosophy, allowing it to endure and evolve over millennia. By grounding his teachings in universal principles of virtue, respect, and harmony, Confucius created a framework that could be applied across cultures and generations.

In essence, Confucius's foundational thought was both deeply personal and profoundly universal. It offered a vision of humanity at its best—compassionate, just, disciplined, and in harmony with the greater order of existence. Through the cultivation of these virtues, individuals could transcend their limitations, creating a world where moral clarity and social harmony prevailed.

These ideas were not merely abstract concepts but living principles, meant to be practiced and embodied in everyday life. They formed the bedrock of a philosophy that would guide not only individuals but entire civilizations, offering a path to navigate the complexities of human existence with wisdom and grace.

Chapter 4
Social Context

The world from which Confucian philosophy emerged was one of profound disarray, a period marked by the collapse of social norms and political structures that had once defined the ancient Chinese way of life. To fully grasp the depth and relevance of Confucius's teachings, it is necessary to delve into the social and political conditions that shaped his era. This context not only inspired his ideas but also laid bare the urgent need for the solutions he proposed.

The decline of the Zhou dynasty was central to the upheaval of the time. Once a unifying force that brought stability and cultural cohesion, the Zhou rulers had gradually lost their ability to maintain order. By the late Spring and Autumn period (770–476 BCE), power had splintered into the hands of feudal lords, each governing their territories with varying degrees of competence and ambition. The Zhou king, nominally at the helm, held little more than symbolic authority, unable to enforce the will of Heaven upon a fractured land.

This political decentralization gave rise to the Warring States period (475–221 BCE), an era defined by relentless conflict and power struggles. Noble families, intoxicated by the allure of expansion and dominance, engaged in constant warfare, often at the expense of their subjects. Armies ravaged the countryside, and communities were uprooted, leaving the common people in a state of vulnerability and despair. The bonds of trust that once connected rulers to the ruled were frayed, threatening the fabric of society itself.

As these conflicts unfolded, the traditional social hierarchy also began to erode. The feudal system, built on clear delineations of rank and duty, crumbled under the weight of greed and opportunism. Loyalty to one's lord or kin was increasingly replaced by alliances of convenience, and the moral expectations that once bound leaders to their people gave way to pragmatism and self-interest. The disintegration of these structures left a moral vacuum, one that Confucius sought to address through his teachings.

Economic pressures compounded these challenges. The advent of new agricultural techniques and the growth of commerce created unprecedented opportunities for wealth, but these developments also deepened social inequalities. While a few prospered, many found themselves trapped in cycles of poverty and exploitation. The resulting tensions added another layer of instability to a society already teetering on the brink.

Amid this turmoil, the lives of ordinary people were marked by uncertainty and suffering. Farmers, artisans, and merchants faced not only the threat of violence but also the unpredictability of their rulers' whims. Tax burdens often fell heaviest on those least able to bear them, and the absence of consistent governance left communities vulnerable to both external attacks and internal strife.

Confucius's philosophy took shape as a response to these conditions. He saw the breakdown of social cohesion as a consequence of moral decay, a loss of the shared values and principles that once guided behavior and governance. For Confucius, the solution was not to impose order through brute force, as the Legalists would later advocate, but to restore it through a return to virtue.

At the core of this vision was the family, which Confucius viewed as the foundational unit of society. He believed that the stability of the state depended on the strength and harmony of familial relationships. The principles of respect, duty, and love cultivated within the family could serve as a model for broader social interactions, creating a ripple effect that extended from the household to the community and, ultimately, to the entire nation.

The Confucian emphasis on filial piety, or Xiao, reflected this belief. For Confucius, the relationship between parent and child was a microcosm of the ideal relationship between ruler and subject. Just as a parent guided their child with wisdom and care, a ruler should lead their people with virtue and compassion. In turn, the child's obedience and respect mirrored the loyalty and trust expected of citizens toward their leaders. This reciprocal relationship was central to Confucian thought, offering a blueprint for rebuilding the trust that had been lost during the Warring States period.

Confucius also recognized the importance of education in addressing the societal challenges of his time. He saw ignorance and moral confusion as key contributors to the chaos around him, and he believed that education was the means by which individuals could be guided back to virtue. Unlike the rigid hierarchies of the feudal system, Confucius's approach to education was inclusive, emphasizing that moral and intellectual growth were attainable for all, regardless of birth or status.

The political landscape of the time posed a formidable challenge to Confucius's ideals. Many rulers were uninterested in virtue, focusing instead on expanding their power and consolidating their resources. The feudal lords, whose legitimacy once stemmed from the Mandate of Heaven, increasingly relied on military might and cunning to assert their dominance. In this environment, Confucius's calls for ethical governance often fell on deaf ears.

Yet Confucius did not waver in his belief that virtue was the cornerstone of effective leadership. He argued that a ruler's moral character was more influential than their laws or decrees. "If the people are led by virtue," he taught, "and uniformity is sought through the practice of ritual, they will develop a sense of shame and come to order of their own accord." In this vision, governance was not about control but about inspiration, with the ruler serving as a moral exemplar for their subjects to emulate.

Confucius's ideas were not without their critics. Some contemporaries dismissed his emphasis on virtue as naive, arguing that strength and strategy were the only paths to stability. Others questioned whether his reverence for tradition could adequately address the complexities of a rapidly changing world. These debates underscored the competing philosophies that emerged during the period, from the mystical detachment of Daoism to the authoritarian pragmatism of Legalism.

Despite these challenges, Confucius's teachings gained a foothold, particularly among those who longed for a return to moral clarity and social harmony. His vision of a society governed by virtue resonated with those disillusioned by the failures of their leaders, offering hope that a better future was possible.

The social context of Confucius's time was both the crucible and the canvas for his philosophy. The chaos and uncertainty of the Warring States period revealed the fragility of human institutions and the enduring need for ethical foundations. Against this backdrop, Confucius crafted a vision of order and harmony rooted not in power but in principle, a vision that sought to heal the fractures of his world by restoring its moral center.

In the face of relentless conflict and moral decay, Confucius did not retreat into abstraction or despair. Instead, he confronted the realities of his time with a profound faith in humanity's capacity for self-correction. He believed that even in the darkest of circumstances, the light of virtue could guide individuals and societies back to balance. His teachings, shaped by the trials of his era, remain a testament to the enduring power of ethical wisdom in the face of adversity.

Chapter 5
Cultural Influences

The philosophy of Confucius did not emerge in isolation; it was deeply shaped by the rich tapestry of cultural traditions, spiritual practices, and intellectual currents of ancient China. To understand the profound impact of Confucianism, one must first examine the cultural milieu that nurtured its development. These influences, ranging from ancestral worship to the concept of Tian (Heaven), provided the foundation upon which Confucius built his vision of a harmonious society.

At the heart of ancient Chinese culture was the practice of ancestor veneration, a tradition that predated Confucius by centuries. This practice, rooted in the belief that the spirits of the deceased could influence the fortunes of the living, emphasized the importance of familial bonds and respect for one's lineage. Families conducted rituals to honor their ancestors, offering sacrifices and prayers to maintain a connection between the past and the present. These rituals reinforced the idea that harmony within the family was integral to the well-being of the broader community.

Confucius adopted and expanded upon this tradition, placing filial piety (Xiao) at the core of his philosophy. For him, the respect shown to one's parents and ancestors was not merely an act of duty but a moral foundation upon which all other virtues were built. The family, he believed, was the first school of virtue, where individuals learned the values of respect, responsibility, and care. This emphasis on familial harmony became a cornerstone of Confucian thought, influencing its approach to ethics, governance, and social order.

Another significant cultural influence on Confucianism was the concept of Tian, often translated as Heaven. In ancient Chinese thought, Tian represented a cosmic order that governed both the natural and human realms. It was both a moral force and a source of legitimacy, granting rulers the Mandate of Heaven as long as they governed with virtue and justice. This belief held that the moral integrity of a ruler was directly tied to the stability of the state, and any deviation from virtuous conduct could result in the loss of divine favor.

Confucius embraced the idea of Tian but reinterpreted it through a moral lens. For him, Tian was not merely a celestial authority but a guiding principle that reflected the ethical structure of the universe. He believed that aligning human behavior with the will of Heaven was essential for achieving harmony, both within individuals and society. This alignment required the cultivation of virtue, which he saw as a means of fulfilling one's moral obligations to both the earthly and celestial realms.

The rituals (Li) that permeated Chinese culture also played a central role in shaping Confucian philosophy. Long before Confucius, ritual practices were integral to maintaining social order and expressing reverence for the divine. These rituals included ceremonies for honoring ancestors, celebrating seasonal changes, and marking significant life events. They were seen as a way to harmonize human actions with the rhythms of nature and the cosmos.

Confucius elevated the importance of rituals, arguing that they were not merely formalities but a means of cultivating moral character and social harmony. He believed that participating in rituals taught individuals discipline, humility, and respect for others. Rituals, in his view, were a bridge between the individual and the collective, reinforcing the values that held society together. Confucius also emphasized the importance of sincerity in performing rituals, insisting that their true value lay in the attitude and intention behind them rather than their outward display.

The Zhou dynasty's emphasis on moral governance and hierarchical relationships also left an indelible mark on Confucianism. The Zhou rulers had established a system of order based on the "Five Relationships," which delineated the roles and responsibilities between ruler and subject, parent and child, husband and wife, elder sibling and younger sibling, and friend and friend. These relationships were hierarchical but reciprocal, requiring both authority and compassion from those in positions of power.

Confucius adopted and refined this framework, using it to articulate his vision of a well-ordered society. He believed that the stability of the state depended on the proper functioning of these relationships, with each individual fulfilling their role with integrity and respect. For example, a ruler's authority was contingent upon their ability to act with virtue and care for their subjects, while subjects were expected to show loyalty and obedience in return. This emphasis on reciprocity and moral responsibility became a defining feature of Confucian thought.

Confucius's philosophy was also shaped by interactions with other schools of thought, such as Daoism and proto-Legalism. Daoist principles of harmony with nature and the pursuit of balance influenced his ideas about the interconnectedness of human relationships and the natural order. While Confucius differed from Daoists in his focus on social structures and rituals, he shared their belief in the importance of aligning human behavior with universal principles.

Proto-Legalist thought, which emphasized strict laws and centralized authority, provided a stark contrast to Confucius's vision of governance. While Legalists sought to impose order through coercion and punishment, Confucius argued that true harmony could only be achieved through the cultivation of virtue. This philosophical tension highlighted the unique moral emphasis of Confucianism, setting it apart as a philosophy rooted in ethical self-cultivation rather than external control.

The influence of ancient Chinese literature and poetry also cannot be overlooked. Confucius held the "Book of Songs"

(Shijing) in high regard, often quoting its verses to illustrate moral principles and inspire reflection. This anthology of poetry, which captured the emotions and experiences of everyday life, resonated with Confucius's belief in the transformative power of art and culture. He saw literature not only as a means of self-expression but as a tool for moral education, capable of nurturing empathy and wisdom.

In addition to these cultural influences, Confucius was deeply attuned to the human condition, drawing insights from the struggles and aspirations of those around him. He observed how the fragmentation of society led to alienation and suffering, and he sought to address these challenges by emphasizing the shared values that united individuals and communities. His philosophy was, in many ways, a response to the cultural and spiritual needs of his time—a vision of renewal that sought to restore balance and harmony in the midst of chaos.

The cultural foundations of Confucianism underscore its enduring relevance. By integrating the traditions of ancestor veneration, the moral guidance of Tian, the discipline of rituals, and the wisdom of literature, Confucius crafted a philosophy that was deeply rooted in the heritage of ancient China. Yet his genius lay in his ability to adapt and reinterpret these traditions, transforming them into a coherent system of thought that addressed the ethical and social challenges of his era.

Through this synthesis, Confucius created a vision of humanity that transcended the particularities of time and place. His philosophy, shaped by the cultural currents of ancient China, remains a testament to the power of tradition as a source of innovation and renewal. By looking to the past, Confucius illuminated a path for the future—one that continues to inspire the pursuit of virtue, harmony, and wisdom in an ever-changing world.

Chapter 6
Classical Texts

At the heart of Confucianism lies a collection of texts that have served as both the foundation and the vessel of its enduring legacy. These works, revered as the "Classics," encapsulate the teachings of Confucius and the broader philosophical, historical, and cultural wisdom of ancient China. Compiled and refined over centuries, the **Four Books** and **Five Classics** offer profound insights into morality, governance, and the human condition, forming a cohesive guide to personal cultivation and social harmony.

The **Four Books—The Analects**, **The Great Learning**, **The Doctrine of the Mean**, and **Mencius**—are central to understanding Confucian thought. These texts were later grouped and emphasized by Zhu Xi, a prominent Confucian scholar of the Song dynasty, but their roots stretch back to Confucius and his immediate disciples. They present the ethical core of Confucianism, emphasizing the cultivation of virtue, the pursuit of wisdom, and the importance of human relationships in achieving harmony.

The Analects, or **Lunyu**, serves as the cornerstone of Confucian philosophy. Compiled by Confucius's disciples after his death, it consists of conversations and reflections that illuminate his teachings on ethics, leadership, and self-cultivation. The text is characterized by its succinct yet profound aphorisms, such as, "The superior man seeks within himself; the inferior man seeks within others." Each passage is a fragment of wisdom, meant to provoke thought and inspire action.

The **Analects** reveal Confucius not as a distant theorist but as a practical teacher, grappling with the moral and social dilemmas of his time. Through its pages, readers encounter his emphasis on Ren (humanity), the transformative power of Li (ritual propriety), and the necessity of leading by example. The text is not merely a collection of ideas but a dialogue, inviting readers to engage with the complexities of ethical life and to apply its lessons to their own circumstances.

The Great Learning, or **Daxue**, provides a roadmap for personal and societal harmony. At its core is the idea that self-cultivation is the foundation of all moral and social order. The text opens with a call to action: "The way of great learning consists in manifesting one's bright virtue, loving the people, and resting in the highest good." This journey begins with introspection and extends outward, linking the individual's moral development to the stability and prosperity of the state.

The emphasis on interconnectedness in **The Great Learning** exemplifies Confucianism's holistic vision. It teaches that only by mastering oneself—through discipline, reflection, and the cultivation of virtue—can one effectively contribute to the greater good. This progression from the personal to the collective underscores the Confucian belief that harmony is not imposed from above but arises organically when individuals align their actions with moral principles.

The Doctrine of the Mean, or **Zhongyong**, explores the concept of balance and moderation. Written as both a philosophical treatise and a guide to ethical living, it emphasizes the importance of finding harmony in all aspects of life. The "mean" refers to a state of equilibrium, achieved by avoiding extremes and cultivating a sense of proportionality in thought and action.

This text introduces the idea of Tianli, or the "Heavenly principle," which serves as the moral compass guiding human behavior. By aligning with this principle, individuals can achieve not only personal harmony but also a sense of unity with the cosmos. The **Doctrine of the Mean** underscores the Confucian ideal of a life lived in accordance with natural and moral laws, a vision of balance that resonates as deeply today as it did in ancient China.

The fourth of the **Four Books**, **Mencius**, expands on Confucius's teachings, offering a more detailed exploration of human nature and political philosophy. Compiled by the eponymous philosopher Mencius (Mengzi), this text argues that humans are inherently good, possessing the seeds of virtue—Ren, Yi, Li, and Zhi (wisdom)—within them. It is through proper cultivation and guidance, Mencius contends, that these seeds can flourish.

Mencius is particularly notable for its reflections on governance. It asserts that rulers must prioritize the welfare of their people and lead with virtue rather than coercion. "The people are the foundation of the state," Mencius declares, emphasizing that the legitimacy of a ruler depends on their ability to act with compassion and justice. This focus on ethical leadership reinforces the Confucian belief in the transformative power of virtue, both at the individual and societal levels.

Complementing the **Four Books** are the **Five Classics**, a collection of ancient texts that provide the historical and cultural context for Confucian philosophy. These works—**The Book of Songs**, **The Book of Documents**, **The Book of Rites**, **The Book of Changes**, and **The Spring and Autumn Annals**—reflect the depth and diversity of Chinese thought, blending poetry, history, and cosmology.

The Book of Songs (Shijing) is a compilation of poetry that captures the emotions and experiences of ancient Chinese life. Its verses, ranging from hymns and folk songs to odes of political critique, offer a glimpse into the values and aspirations of the Zhou dynasty. For Confucius, these poems were more than literary expressions; they were tools for moral education, teaching empathy, virtue, and an appreciation for beauty.

The Book of Documents (Shujing) is a collection of speeches, decrees, and historical accounts, chronicling the governance of early Chinese rulers. It emphasizes the moral responsibilities of leadership, illustrating how virtue and justice can sustain the Mandate of Heaven. Confucius regarded these records as examples of ethical governance, using them to inspire his vision of a morally grounded political order.

The Book of Rites (Liji) delves into the rituals and customs that underpin social harmony. It outlines the proper conduct for individuals in various roles and situations, from family life to state ceremonies. For Confucius, these rituals were not mere formalities but a means of cultivating discipline, respect, and a sense of connection to the past and future.

The Book of Changes (Yijing) is a cosmological and divinatory text that explores the interplay of yin and yang, the fundamental forces of the universe. Its hexagrams, composed of broken and unbroken lines, represent the dynamic patterns of change that govern all existence. While the text's mystical elements may seem at odds with Confucian pragmatism, Confucius valued its insights into balance and adaptability, integrating them into his understanding of harmony.

The Spring and Autumn Annals (Chunqiu) is a historical chronicle attributed to Confucius himself. It records events in the state of Lu, offering a moral commentary on the actions of rulers and statesmen. This work reflects Confucius's belief in the importance of history as a guide to ethical decision-making, highlighting the consequences of virtue and vice in governance.

Together, the **Four Books** and **Five Classics** form the intellectual foundation of Confucianism. They are not merely texts to be studied but living guides, meant to shape the character and actions of those who engage with them. Through their wisdom, Confucianism bridges the past and the present, offering timeless principles for navigating the complexities of human existence.

These texts, revered across millennia, reveal the profound depth and breadth of Confucian thought. They invite readers not only to understand the teachings of Confucius but to embody them, transforming knowledge into action and creating a world guided by virtue, harmony, and wisdom.

Chapter 7
The Confucian School

The emergence of the Confucian school was neither instantaneous nor effortless. It was the product of a deliberate effort by Confucius's disciples to preserve, systematize, and expand his teachings. This process began in the years following Confucius's death in 479 BCE, as his immediate followers grappled with the task of ensuring that his vision would not fade into obscurity. The early formation of the Confucian school was marked by the interplay of loyalty to the master's ideals and the need to adapt those ideals to the evolving challenges of their time.

At the heart of this endeavor were Confucius's disciples, a diverse group united by their commitment to his vision of virtue and harmony. These men came from varying social and economic backgrounds, reflecting Confucius's belief that education and moral development were not the exclusive domain of the elite. Their shared dedication to the master's teachings was the foundation upon which the Confucian school—known as **Ru Jia**, or the School of the Scholars—was built.

Among the most prominent of these disciples was **Yan Hui**, often regarded as Confucius's favorite student. Yan Hui exemplified the virtues that Confucius prized most: humility, diligence, and an unwavering commitment to self-cultivation. Though his life was tragically cut short, Yan Hui's devotion to his master's teachings left a profound impact on the Confucian tradition. He became a symbol of the ideal disciple, embodying the virtues that Confucius sought to instill in all who followed his path.

Another key figure was **Zengzi**, whose reflections on filial piety and moral integrity became integral to Confucian thought.

Zengzi's teachings emphasized the importance of introspection and the cultivation of one's inner moral compass, ideas that would resonate throughout the Confucian tradition. He was also credited with contributing to the development of the **Great Learning**, one of the foundational texts of Confucianism.

Zilu, known for his bold and passionate nature, represented a different aspect of the Confucian school. While his temperament sometimes clashed with Confucius's preference for moderation, Zilu's courage and loyalty earned him a place of respect among the master's disciples. His life illustrated the challenges of applying Confucian principles in a turbulent world, highlighting the tension between idealism and pragmatism that would continue to shape the Confucian school.

After Confucius's death, his disciples began the work of compiling his teachings into a coherent body of knowledge. This effort resulted in the creation of the **Analects**, a collection of Confucius's sayings and dialogues. The **Analects** became the cornerstone of the Confucian school, preserving the master's wisdom while allowing future generations to engage with his ideas.

The disciples also sought to expand upon Confucius's teachings, addressing the pressing issues of their time through the lens of his philosophy. This process of interpretation and adaptation marked the beginning of a dynamic tradition that would evolve over centuries. As the disciples traveled across China, sharing their master's vision with rulers and scholars, they laid the groundwork for the Confucian school's enduring influence.

The Confucian school's development was further shaped by the contributions of later thinkers, most notably **Mencius** and **Xunzi**, who built upon and refined Confucius's teachings. These two figures, while both committed to the Confucian vision, represented distinct interpretations of its core principles, highlighting the diversity and adaptability of the tradition.

Mencius, born more than a century after Confucius, was a passionate advocate for the innate goodness of human nature. He argued that every individual possesses the seeds of virtue—compassion, righteousness, propriety, and wisdom—and that these seeds can flourish through proper cultivation. Mencius's writings emphasized the importance of education and moral leadership, asserting that a ruler's legitimacy depended on their ability to care for the well-being of their people. His work expanded the Confucian school's focus on governance, linking the cultivation of individual virtue to the stability and prosperity of the state.

In contrast, **Xunzi**, who lived during the later Warring States period, took a more pragmatic view of human nature. He contended that people are born with selfish tendencies and that virtue must be cultivated through discipline, education, and the enforcement of social norms. Xunzi placed a greater emphasis on the role of rituals and institutions in shaping moral behavior, arguing that the Confucian vision of harmony could only be achieved through deliberate effort and collective responsibility.

While their perspectives differed, both Mencius and Xunzi contributed to the Confucian school's intellectual richness. Their debates on human nature, governance, and morality reflected the school's commitment to addressing the complexities of human existence, ensuring its relevance in a rapidly changing world.

The institutionalization of the Confucian school began during the Han dynasty (206 BCE–220 CE), when Confucianism was adopted as the official state ideology. Under Emperor Wu, the state established academies to promote Confucian education, and the **Five Classics** became the foundation of the imperial examination system. This integration of Confucian principles into the fabric of governance marked a turning point in the school's history, transforming it from a philosophical tradition into a guiding force for Chinese civilization.

The early Confucian school also faced challenges and competition from other philosophical traditions, such as Daoism and Legalism. Daoism's emphasis on spontaneity and alignment with nature offered an alternative to Confucianism's focus on social structures and rituals, while Legalism's emphasis on strict laws and centralized authority appealed to rulers seeking immediate solutions to political instability. These competing philosophies forced the Confucian school to articulate and defend its vision, refining its ideas through dialogue and debate.

Despite these challenges, the Confucian school endured, adapting to the changing needs of society while remaining true to its core principles. Its emphasis on education, moral leadership, and the cultivation of virtue provided a framework for addressing the social and political challenges of its time, and its legacy continues to inspire efforts toward harmony and ethical governance.

The formation of the Confucian school was not merely an academic endeavor; it was a testament to the enduring power of Confucius's vision. Through the efforts of his disciples and their successors, the school became a living tradition, evolving in response to new challenges while remaining rooted in the timeless principles of virtue and harmony.

The Confucian school's early development offers a profound lesson: that the pursuit of wisdom is not a solitary journey but a collective effort, sustained by the contributions of those who seek to embody and transmit its teachings. By preserving and expanding Confucius's vision, the school ensured that his ideas would continue to shape the course of history, offering guidance and inspiration to generations yet to come.

Chapter 8
The Philosophical Tradition

The evolution of Confucianism from its early roots into a central philosophical tradition in Chinese history reflects both the resilience of its core principles and its capacity to adapt across centuries. This journey began with the foundational teachings of Confucius and his immediate disciples but grew into a dynamic and expansive tradition that influenced governance, education, and morality on a vast scale. The Confucian philosophical tradition became a cornerstone of Chinese civilization, shaping the moral fabric of society and leaving an indelible mark on the cultures of East Asia.

In its earliest form, Confucianism was not a rigid doctrine but a flexible and evolving set of ideas, grounded in the belief that harmony—both personal and societal—could be achieved through the cultivation of virtue. The early Confucian thinkers preserved this vision while expanding its scope, offering responses to the changing political, social, and cultural conditions of their times. This ability to evolve while remaining true to its core principles became a defining feature of the Confucian tradition.

The **Han dynasty** (206 BCE–220 CE) marked a turning point in the history of Confucianism. Under Emperor Wu, Confucianism was adopted as the state's official ideology, becoming the foundation for governance and education. The imperial court established Confucian academies, and the **Five Classics** were enshrined as the basis of the civil service examinations, which determined entry into the government bureaucracy. This institutionalization of Confucianism ensured its survival and influence, embedding its principles into the structure of Chinese society.

During the Han period, Confucianism also absorbed elements from other philosophical traditions, such as Daoism and Yin-Yang cosmology. This synthesis enriched the tradition, allowing it to address a broader range of questions about human existence and the natural world. The integration of cosmological ideas into Confucian thought deepened its metaphysical dimensions, linking the cultivation of virtue to the harmonious functioning of the universe.

Following the Han dynasty, Confucianism faced significant challenges as China entered a period of political fragmentation and cultural upheaval. The rise of Buddhism during the **Six Dynasties** (220–589 CE) introduced new religious and philosophical perspectives that competed with Confucianism for influence. Buddhism's emphasis on spiritual enlightenment and its critique of worldly attachments appealed to many during this era of instability, prompting Confucian scholars to reconsider and refine their ideas.

This period of competition and dialogue gave rise to a reinvigoration of the Confucian tradition. Scholars began to engage with Buddhist and Daoist ideas, integrating their insights into Confucian thought while reaffirming its commitment to ethical and social principles. This intellectual exchange set the stage for the emergence of **Neo-Confucianism** during the **Song dynasty** (960–1279 CE).

Neo-Confucianism represented a major philosophical development within the Confucian tradition, led by figures such as **Zhou Dunyi**, **Zhang Zai**, **Cheng Hao**, **Cheng Yi**, and **Zhu Xi**. These thinkers sought to address metaphysical and spiritual questions that earlier Confucians had left largely unexplored, drawing inspiration from both Buddhist and Daoist ideas while remaining firmly rooted in Confucian values.

At the heart of Neo-Confucianism was the concept of **Li** (principle) and **Qi** (vital energy). Li was understood as the underlying order of the universe, the rational structure that governed all existence. Qi, by contrast, referred to the material and dynamic force that animated the world. Together, these concepts offered a comprehensive framework for understanding the relationship between the individual, society, and the cosmos.

Zhu Xi, the most influential Neo-Confucian thinker, systematized these ideas into a cohesive philosophical system. He emphasized the importance of introspection, study, and self-cultivation as pathways to understanding Li and achieving harmony with the cosmic order. Zhu Xi also redefined the Confucian canon, elevating the **Four Books** to a central position in the tradition. His commentaries on these texts became authoritative guides for generations of scholars and officials.

Neo-Confucianism extended Confucianism's influence beyond the boundaries of China, shaping the intellectual and cultural landscapes of Korea, Japan, and Vietnam. In Korea, thinkers such as **Yi Hwang** (Toegye) and **Yi I** (Yulgok) adapted Neo-Confucian principles to local contexts, influencing governance and education. In Japan, Confucianism informed the ethical foundations of the Tokugawa shogunate, contributing to the development of Bushido, the samurai code of conduct. Vietnam, too, embraced Confucian ideals, integrating them into its political and educational systems.

Despite its institutional success, Confucianism was not immune to criticism. During the late imperial period, thinkers began to question its relevance in the face of new challenges, such as the increasing complexity of bureaucratic governance and the arrival of Western ideas. Critics argued that the rigid application of Confucian principles sometimes stifled innovation and perpetuated social inequalities.

The arrival of modernity in the 19th and 20th centuries brought further challenges to the Confucian tradition. The decline of the Qing dynasty, the rise of republicanism, and the spread of Western science and philosophy led many to view Confucianism as outdated and incompatible with the demands of the modern world. Revolutionary movements in China, including the May Fourth Movement and the Communist Revolution, often portrayed Confucianism as a symbol of feudal oppression and sought to dismantle its influence.

Yet even in the face of these challenges, Confucianism proved remarkably resilient. Scholars and thinkers continued to engage with its principles, reinterpreting them in light of contemporary concerns. The 20th century saw a revival of interest in Confucianism, as intellectuals sought to reconcile its ethical insights with modern values such as democracy, equality, and human rights. This revival, often referred to as **New Confucianism**, emphasized the universal relevance of Confucian principles, presenting them as a moral framework for addressing global challenges.

Today, Confucianism continues to inspire philosophical inquiry and practical action. In China, the government has embraced aspects of Confucian thought as part of its cultural heritage, promoting values such as social harmony and respect for tradition. Across East Asia, Confucian principles remain integral to educational systems, family structures, and societal norms. Beyond its historical heartland, Confucianism has gained recognition as a source of wisdom for addressing contemporary issues, from environmental sustainability to ethical leadership.

The Confucian philosophical tradition is a testament to the enduring power of ideas that speak to the core of human experience. Rooted in the teachings of a single man, it has grown into a rich and multifaceted tradition that transcends time and place. Its emphasis on virtue, harmony, and the interconnectedness of all things offers a vision of life that remains as compelling today as it was in ancient China.

Through its evolution, Confucianism has shown that a commitment to ethical principles need not be static or inflexible. Instead, it can be a living tradition, continually adapting to new challenges while remaining true to its foundational ideals. This ability to bridge past and present, individual and collective, is the essence of the Confucian legacy—a legacy that invites all who encounter it to reflect, to cultivate, and to strive for a life of greater meaning and purpose.

Chapter 9
Essential Virtue

At the heart of Confucian thought lies the concept of **Dé** (virtue), a central principle that defines the moral character and guiding force of individuals, families, and societies. In the Confucian worldview, Dé is not merely an abstract notion but an active quality that permeates all aspects of life. It is the foundation upon which moral actions, harmonious relationships, and effective governance are built. Confucius regarded Dé as the cornerstone of humanity's potential, a force capable of transforming both the individual and the world around them.

Dé is expansive in its scope, encompassing various attributes such as integrity, benevolence, righteousness, and wisdom. It is both a personal and collective virtue, cultivated through self-discipline and expressed through actions that align with moral principles. In Confucian philosophy, the cultivation of Dé begins within the individual, radiates outward to influence familial relationships, and ultimately extends to society at large. This progression from self to community forms the backbone of Confucian ethics.

Confucius described Dé as a magnetic force, one that naturally draws others toward the virtuous individual. He famously said, "He who governs by virtue is like the North Star: it remains in its place, and all the stars turn toward it." This metaphor illustrates the transformative power of Dé, portraying it as a stabilizing and unifying influence. For Confucius, a virtuous person does not need to impose authority through coercion or fear; their moral example is sufficient to inspire others to follow their lead.

The cultivation of Dé begins with **self-cultivation**, a practice that Confucius regarded as both a moral obligation and a lifelong pursuit. Self-cultivation involves a deliberate effort to align one's thoughts, words, and actions with ethical principles. It requires constant introspection, discipline, and a willingness to confront one's flaws. Confucius taught that the path to virtue is not always easy, but it is accessible to anyone willing to undertake the journey.

Central to self-cultivation is the practice of **Zheng Xin**, or the rectification of the mind. This involves developing clarity and sincerity in one's intentions, ensuring that actions are motivated by genuine concern for others rather than selfish desires. Confucius believed that a person's inner state profoundly influences their external behavior; by purifying the heart and mind, one can act with integrity and compassion.

The role of education in cultivating Dé cannot be overstated. For Confucius, education was not merely a means of acquiring knowledge but a process of moral refinement. He emphasized the importance of studying the classics, engaging in dialogue with others, and reflecting on personal experiences to deepen one's understanding of virtue. Education, in the Confucian sense, is a transformative practice that shapes not only the intellect but also the character.

The expression of Dé is most evident in interpersonal relationships. Confucius stressed that virtue is not an isolated quality but one that manifests in the way individuals treat others. The concept of **Ren** (humanity or benevolence) is closely tied to Dé, representing the compassionate aspect of virtue. A person with Ren demonstrates kindness, empathy, and a genuine concern for the well-being of others.

Confucius's teachings on Ren emphasize the reciprocal nature of human relationships. He often invoked the Golden Rule, advising, "Do not impose on others what you do not wish for yourself." This principle underscores the interconnectedness of all individuals, suggesting that the cultivation of Dé is incomplete without a commitment to fostering harmony within one's community.

In the family, Dé finds expression through **Xiao** (filial piety), the virtue of respecting and honoring one's parents and ancestors. Filial piety is regarded as the root of all virtue, serving as the foundation for ethical behavior in all other relationships. Confucius taught that the values learned within the family—respect, responsibility, and care—form the basis for moral conduct in society. By practicing Xiao, individuals contribute to the stability and harmony of both their households and the broader community.

Beyond the family, Dé extends to the realm of governance. Confucius envisioned a society in which rulers governed not through force or fear but through moral authority. He argued that the legitimacy of a ruler depended on their ability to embody Dé, inspiring loyalty and trust among their subjects. "The ruler who governs with virtue," Confucius said, "is like the wind, while the people are like the grass. When the wind blows, the grass bends." This analogy highlights the profound influence of a virtuous leader, whose moral example shapes the behavior of the governed.

In Confucian thought, a ruler's Dé is not only a personal quality but also a reflection of the **Mandate of Heaven** (Tianming). According to this principle, Heaven grants authority to those who govern with virtue and withdraws it from those who fail to uphold moral principles. This belief served as both an inspiration and a constraint for rulers, reminding them that their power was conditional upon their adherence to ethical governance.

While Dé is often associated with leadership, Confucius emphasized that it is a universal quality, one that every individual has the capacity to cultivate. He rejected the notion that virtue was an inherent trait or the exclusive privilege of the elite. Instead, he argued that Dé could be developed through conscious effort and practice, regardless of one's social status or background.

Confucius's teachings on Dé were further elaborated by later thinkers such as **Mencius** and **Xunzi**, who offered differing perspectives on its origins and cultivation. Mencius argued that virtue is innate, a natural expression of the goodness within every human being. He believed that Dé flourishes when individuals nurture their inherent tendencies toward compassion and justice.

In contrast, Xunzi took a more pragmatic view, asserting that virtue must be cultivated through discipline and education. He contended that human nature is inherently self-serving and that Dé arises from the deliberate effort to overcome these tendencies. While their views diverged, both Mencius and Xunzi affirmed the transformative power of Dé and its central role in Confucian ethics.

The relevance of Dé extends beyond the historical context of Confucianism. Its emphasis on integrity, empathy, and moral leadership offers valuable insights for addressing the challenges of contemporary life. In an era marked by social fragmentation and ethical dilemmas, the cultivation of Dé provides a framework for building trust, fostering cooperation, and promoting the common good.

Dé is not static; it is a dynamic and evolving quality that requires continuous effort and reflection. It challenges individuals to transcend their limitations, to act with courage and compassion, and to strive for harmony in their relationships and communities. Through its cultivation, Confucianism teaches, humanity can realize its highest potential, creating a world where virtue guides every aspect of life.

As the essence of Confucian thought, Dé remains a timeless ideal, a beacon of hope and wisdom that illuminates the path toward a more just and harmonious existence. Its enduring power lies in its simplicity: the belief that by cultivating virtue within ourselves, we can transform the world around us, fostering a legacy of goodness that transcends generations.

Chapter 10
True Humanity

At the core of Confucianism lies the concept of **Ren** (humanity or benevolence), regarded as the highest and most encompassing virtue. Ren is the essence of what it means to be human—a profound sense of compassion, empathy, and altruism that guides individuals to act in harmony with others. For Confucius, Ren was not only the foundation of ethical conduct but also the ultimate goal of self-cultivation. To embody Ren is to achieve moral excellence and to contribute to the creation of a just and harmonious society.

Ren is often described as the virtue of virtues, the quality that binds all others together. Confucius himself offered a simple yet profound explanation: "Ren means to love others." Yet, this love is not a passive sentiment; it is an active and deliberate choice to care for the well-being of others and to act with integrity and kindness. Ren encompasses a deep understanding of interconnectedness, the realization that individual actions ripple outward to affect families, communities, and the broader world.

The cultivation of Ren begins with the self. Confucius emphasized that before one can extend compassion to others, they must first cultivate a sense of inner harmony and moral clarity. This process involves constant self-reflection, as captured in his famous teaching: "Each day, I examine myself on three points: Have I been unfaithful in my duties to others? Have I been untrustworthy in my words? Have I failed to practice what I teach?" Through such introspection, individuals can identify and correct their shortcomings, aligning their actions with the principles of Ren.

Ren also requires the practice of **Shu** (reciprocity), often expressed as the Golden Rule: "Do not impose on others what you do not wish for yourself." Shu serves as a practical guideline for achieving Ren, encouraging individuals to consider the perspectives and needs of others in their actions. It reflects the mutual respect and empathy that lie at the heart of human relationships. By practicing Shu, individuals learn to transcend selfishness and cultivate a sense of shared humanity.

In the family, Ren manifests as **Xiao** (filial piety), the devotion and respect that children owe to their parents and ancestors. Confucius viewed Xiao as the root of Ren, a virtue that teaches individuals to recognize and honor the interconnectedness of generations. By caring for one's parents and fulfilling familial obligations, individuals develop the qualities of empathy and responsibility that are essential for practicing Ren in broader social contexts.

Beyond the family, Ren extends to all human relationships, shaping the way individuals interact with friends, neighbors, colleagues, and strangers. Confucius often spoke of Ren as a dynamic quality, one that must adapt to the context and demands of each situation. He taught that true humanity is expressed not only in grand gestures but also in the small acts of kindness and consideration that build trust and harmony in daily life.

In governance, Ren plays a pivotal role in Confucius's vision of ethical leadership. He argued that rulers must embody Ren, leading not through coercion but through moral example. A ruler who practices Ren inspires loyalty and respect, creating a stable and harmonious society. Confucius declared, "If a ruler has Ren, what difficulty will he have in governing? If he does not have Ren, what use will ritual propriety (Li) be to him?" This teaching highlights the interconnectedness of Ren with other Confucian virtues, such as Li (ritual) and Yi (justice).

Ren also serves as a unifying principle, bridging the gap between personal morality and societal harmony. It encourages individuals to act not out of self-interest but with a sense of responsibility toward the greater good. Confucius envisioned a society where Ren was the guiding force, a world in which individuals worked together to create an environment of mutual care and respect.

However, achieving Ren is not without challenges. Confucius acknowledged that the cultivation of humanity requires effort, discipline, and courage. He taught that Ren demands more than passive goodwill; it calls for action, even in the face of adversity. "The way of Ren is difficult," he admitted, "but it is the path worth walking." This difficulty is what makes Ren so transformative—by striving to embody it, individuals elevate themselves and those around them.

The practice of Ren requires a delicate balance between compassion and discernment. While it calls for empathy and kindness, it also demands the ability to make ethical judgments and to act with integrity. Confucius warned against the dangers of indulgence, emphasizing that true humanity involves not only caring for others but also guiding them toward virtue. This balance reflects the holistic nature of Ren, which integrates emotional warmth with moral strength.

Ren's universality is one of its most remarkable qualities. It transcends cultural and temporal boundaries, resonating with the shared human aspiration for connection and harmony. Confucius's teachings on Ren have inspired countless individuals and societies, offering a framework for navigating the complexities of human relationships. Whether in personal interactions or global diplomacy, the principles of Ren remain relevant, reminding us of the power of empathy and cooperation.

Later Confucian thinkers, such as **Mencius**, further elaborated on the concept of Ren. Mencius emphasized that Ren is rooted in human nature, an innate capacity for compassion that must be nurtured through education and practice. He illustrated this idea with the example of a child falling into a well: any person who witnesses such an event, Mencius argued, would feel an instinctive urge to save the child. This natural empathy, he claimed, is the seed of Ren, a potential that can flourish through cultivation.

In contrast, **Xunzi** took a more pragmatic view, arguing that Ren is not inherent but must be developed through deliberate effort and discipline. He believed that human beings are naturally inclined toward selfishness and that the cultivation of Ren requires the guidance of rituals, laws, and education. While their perspectives differed, both Mencius and Xunzi recognized the transformative power of Ren and its central role in Confucian ethics.

Ren's influence extends beyond Confucianism, finding echoes in other philosophical and religious traditions. Its emphasis on compassion and reciprocity resonates with the teachings of Buddhism, Christianity, and Islam, underscoring its universal appeal. This shared focus on humanity highlights the interconnectedness of moral traditions, offering a common ground for dialogue and cooperation.

In the modern world, the principles of Ren offer valuable insights for addressing contemporary challenges. From building inclusive communities to fostering global understanding, the practice of true humanity is essential for creating a more just and harmonious society. Ren reminds us that our shared humanity transcends divisions, encouraging us to act with compassion and respect in all aspects of life.

Ultimately, Ren is not a destination but a journey—a lifelong commitment to becoming the best version of oneself while uplifting others. It is the embodiment of Confucius's belief in the potential for human goodness, a vision of a world where virtue and kindness prevail. Through the cultivation of Ren, individuals can transform themselves and their societies, creating a legacy of compassion that endures across generations.

Confucius's teachings on Ren remain a timeless call to action, inviting each of us to embrace our shared humanity and to strive for a life guided by love, empathy, and integrity. In a world often marked by division and strife, Ren offers a path toward unity, reminding us of the profound truth that to be truly human is to care for one another.

Chapter 11
Natural Justice

Confucianism elevates the concept of **Yi** (justice or righteousness) to a position of profound importance, framing it as an essential virtue that enables individuals to discern and act in accordance with moral principles. Unlike laws that impose order through external force, Yi emanates from within, guiding individuals to choose the path of integrity even when faced with challenges or temptations. It is a virtue that transcends personal gain, standing as a testament to the moral strength of the human spirit.

In the Confucian tradition, Yi is not merely about adherence to rules but reflects a deeper alignment with what is ethically correct. It requires the capacity to assess situations, weigh their moral implications, and act in a way that upholds fairness and honor. For Confucius, the essence of Yi was encapsulated in his teachings: "The superior man understands righteousness, while the inferior man understands profit." This distinction underscores the selflessness at the heart of Yi, contrasting it with the pursuit of material or selfish interests.

The cultivation of Yi begins with the ability to distinguish right from wrong, a skill that Confucius believed was rooted in self-cultivation and education. Through reflection and study, individuals develop the moral clarity necessary to navigate complex situations. Yi is not static; it is a dynamic virtue that must be exercised and refined through practice. In every decision, the individual is called to rise above personal biases and to act in harmony with the greater good.

Yi is closely intertwined with other Confucian virtues, particularly **Ren** (humanity) and **Li** (ritual propriety). While Ren emphasizes compassion and empathy, Yi ensures that this compassion is directed toward just outcomes. Similarly, Li provides a framework for orderly conduct, but it is Yi that determines whether adherence to rituals serves the cause of righteousness. Together, these virtues form a cohesive moral system, each reinforcing and balancing the others.

The practical application of Yi is especially significant in decision-making. Confucius emphasized that righteousness often demands difficult choices, requiring individuals to prioritize ethical principles over convenience or personal gain. This might involve standing against corruption, defending the vulnerable, or upholding fairness in the face of adversity. Yi, therefore, is not an abstract ideal but a lived reality that manifests in actions large and small.

Historical accounts illustrate the power of Yi in action. One notable example is the story of **Bo Yi** and **Shu Qi**, two brothers who chose to abandon their claim to their father's throne, believing that it was unjust to seek power for themselves. Their commitment to righteousness, even at great personal cost, became a symbol of moral integrity in Confucian thought. Such stories highlight the transformative potential of Yi, inspiring individuals to align their actions with higher principles.

Yi also plays a crucial role in governance, shaping the Confucian vision of ethical leadership. Confucius argued that a ruler guided by Yi creates a just and harmonious society, setting an example for their subjects to follow. He believed that laws and punishments were secondary to the moral authority of a virtuous leader, whose actions naturally inspire trust and respect. "Govern the people by regulations," Confucius warned, "and they will evade them. Lead them by virtue and justice, and they will reform themselves."

The relationship between Yi and justice extends to the legal and social structures of society. In Confucian thought, justice is not merely about enforcing rules but about ensuring that fairness prevails. This requires sensitivity to context, as rigid adherence to laws can sometimes conflict with the principles of Yi. For example, Confucius taught that rituals and rules should not be applied mechanically but should serve the broader purpose of fostering harmony and righteousness.

Yi also informs the Confucian approach to conflict resolution. In disputes, the goal is not simply to determine who is right or wrong but to restore balance and harmony. This perspective reflects the holistic nature of Confucian ethics, which seeks to address not only the immediate problem but also the underlying relationships and values at stake. Yi guides individuals to seek solutions that honor both justice and compassion, promoting reconciliation rather than division.

The cultivation of Yi is a lifelong process, one that requires constant reflection and effort. Confucius encouraged his disciples to develop the habit of examining their actions and motivations, asking themselves whether they had acted in accordance with righteousness. This practice of self-scrutiny fosters a deep sense of accountability, ensuring that one's choices are guided by principles rather than impulses.

While Confucius laid the foundation for the concept of Yi, later Confucian thinkers expanded on its significance. **Mencius**, for example, emphasized the connection between Yi and human nature, arguing that the capacity for righteousness is innate but must be nurtured through education and moral cultivation. He famously compared Yi to the instinctive feeling of compassion one would have for a child in danger, suggesting that righteousness is a natural extension of humanity's empathetic tendencies.

Xunzi, on the other hand, offered a more structured approach to Yi, emphasizing the importance of discipline and social institutions in shaping moral behavior. He argued that while individuals are not inherently righteous, they can develop Yi through the deliberate practice of virtues and adherence to rituals. His perspective highlights the role of external guidance in complementing internal moral effort.

The relevance of Yi extends beyond its historical and cultural origins. In contemporary society, its principles offer a powerful framework for addressing ethical dilemmas and promoting social justice. Whether in leadership, education, or interpersonal relationships, Yi challenges individuals to act with integrity and to prioritize the common good over personal gain. Its emphasis on fairness and moral clarity provides a counterbalance to the complexities and ambiguities of modern life.

In the realm of leadership, Yi remains a vital standard for evaluating actions and policies. Leaders guided by righteousness prioritize the welfare of their people, making decisions that reflect both fairness and compassion. This approach fosters trust and cooperation, creating a foundation for sustainable and equitable governance. In contrast, the absence of Yi leads to corruption, exploitation, and social fragmentation, underscoring its importance as a guiding principle.

Yi also holds profound implications for personal growth. By striving to embody righteousness, individuals cultivate a sense of purpose and resilience, enabling them to navigate life's challenges with confidence and integrity. The practice of Yi encourages self-improvement not for the sake of personal gain but for the benefit of others, reinforcing the interconnectedness of individual and collective well-being.

Ultimately, Yi is more than a virtue; it is a way of life, a commitment to living in alignment with ethical principles and contributing to the creation of a just and harmonious world. Its transformative power lies in its ability to inspire individuals to transcend their limitations and to act as agents of righteousness in their communities.

Confucianism teaches that righteousness is not merely an ideal to be admired but a force to be embodied and enacted. Yi calls each of us to recognize our capacity for moral courage and to use that capacity to make choices that uphold fairness and integrity. In doing so, we not only honor the legacy of Confucian thought but also contribute to a more just and compassionate society, one where righteousness prevails and harmony endures.

Chapter 12
Sacred Rituals

In Confucianism, **Li** (ritual propriety) emerges as one of the most profound and practical concepts, weaving together the threads of morality, tradition, and social order. Far from being mere ceremonial acts, Li encompasses a vast spectrum of behaviors, customs, and protocols that guide individuals in their interactions with others and with the world. At its core, Li is the discipline through which individuals cultivate their inner virtue and contribute to the harmony of society.

Confucius regarded Li as a cornerstone of a well-ordered life, teaching that rituals, when performed with sincerity, reflect and reinforce moral character. He stated, "Rituals performed without sincerity are as though not performed at all." This insight underscores that the value of rituals lies not in their outward performance but in the intentionality and respect they embody. Through Li, the mundane becomes meaningful, and everyday actions acquire a sacred dimension.

Historically, Li has its roots in ancient Chinese traditions, particularly in the practices of ancestor veneration and offerings to Tian (Heaven). These rituals expressed a deep reverence for the forces that shaped human existence, serving as a bridge between the earthly and the divine. Confucius inherited these traditions and expanded their significance, framing Li as a tool not only for spiritual connection but also for cultivating personal virtue and social cohesion.

Li begins with the individual, shaping behavior and fostering self-discipline. Confucius taught that through the practice of rituals, one learns to temper desires, control impulses, and align one's actions with ethical principles. Rituals, whether simple or elaborate, act as constant reminders of one's responsibilities to others and to the broader moral order. For example, acts as simple as bowing in greeting or offering thanks reinforce humility and respect, qualities that lie at the heart of Confucian ethics.

In the family, Li plays a vital role in nurturing harmony and reinforcing bonds. Rituals such as ancestral rites and familial celebrations honor the interconnectedness of generations, instilling a sense of continuity and shared purpose. Confucius emphasized that these rituals are not just about honoring the past but also about cultivating the present. By observing family rituals, individuals deepen their understanding of respect, gratitude, and their place within the broader social fabric.

One of the most significant expressions of Li within the family is the observance of **funerary rites**. These rituals, marked by solemnity and reverence, reflect the Confucian belief in honoring the departed as a way of maintaining harmony between the living and the deceased. Funerary practices are seen as an opportunity to express gratitude, uphold filial piety, and strengthen familial bonds. Confucius believed that through such acts, individuals cultivated their sense of humanity and moral responsibility.

In society, Li serves as the foundation for ethical interactions and social stability. Confucius taught that rituals create a sense of order and predictability, enabling individuals to navigate their relationships with clarity and respect. Whether in formal ceremonies or everyday exchanges, Li provides a framework for behavior that fosters trust, mutual understanding, and harmony. For instance, the rituals observed during marriage ceremonies, diplomatic negotiations, or community gatherings symbolize the values of commitment, cooperation, and unity.

The transformative power of Li lies in its ability to elevate ordinary actions into meaningful expressions of virtue. Confucius illustrated this with his meticulous attention to detail in rituals, emphasizing that every gesture, no matter how small, carries moral significance. He believed that by perfecting one's conduct in rituals, individuals develop the habits and attitudes that define a virtuous life.

Li also extends to the realm of governance, where it plays a crucial role in Confucian political philosophy. For Confucius, a ruler who embodies Li demonstrates their commitment to justice, humility, and the welfare of the people. Rituals in governance are not mere formalities but acts of moral leadership, designed to inspire loyalty and respect. By performing their duties with propriety, rulers set an example for their subjects, fostering a culture of virtue and accountability.

In the context of governance, **sacrificial rites** held particular significance. These ceremonies, conducted in honor of Heaven, ancestors, and nature, symbolized the ruler's alignment with cosmic order and their responsibility to uphold harmony within the state. Confucius believed that such rituals reinforced the moral legitimacy of leadership, serving as a reminder that power must be exercised with virtue and integrity.

While Confucius placed great emphasis on tradition, he also recognized the need for flexibility and adaptation in the practice of Li. He taught that rituals should evolve to reflect the values and needs of the time, cautioning against rigid adherence to outdated customs. This perspective highlights the dynamic nature of Li, which balances reverence for the past with responsiveness to the present.

The integration of Li with other Confucian virtues further illustrates its holistic role in ethical life. While Ren (humanity) inspires compassion and empathy, Li provides the structure through which these qualities are expressed. Similarly, Yi (justice) ensures that rituals are guided by righteousness, preventing them from becoming hollow formalities. Together, these virtues create a moral framework that is both principled and practical.

Later Confucian thinkers elaborated on the concept of Li, exploring its philosophical and metaphysical dimensions. **Zhu Xi**, a leading figure of Neo-Confucianism, emphasized the connection between Li and the underlying principles of the universe. He argued that rituals reflect the natural order, serving as a means of aligning human behavior with cosmic harmony. This interpretation enriched the Confucian understanding of Li, linking it to broader questions of existence and purpose.

Despite its ancient origins, the principles of Li remain deeply relevant in the modern world. In a time marked by rapid change and social fragmentation, the practice of rituals offers a way to reconnect with tradition, build community, and foster a sense of belonging. Whether through cultural celebrations, civic ceremonies, or simple acts of courtesy, Li provides a framework for creating meaningful and respectful interactions.

In professional and interpersonal contexts, Li serves as a reminder of the importance of ethical behavior and mutual respect. Practices such as acknowledging contributions, adhering to ethical standards, and observing protocols reflect the spirit of Li, demonstrating that rituals continue to play a vital role in shaping character and building trust.

Ultimately, Li is a practice of alignment—between individuals and their communities, between the present and the past, and between humanity and the natural order. It teaches that rituals are not ends in themselves but pathways to greater understanding and harmony. Through the disciplined practice of Li, individuals cultivate their inner virtue and contribute to the collective good, embodying the Confucian vision of a life guided by respect, responsibility, and reverence.

Confucius's teachings on Li remain a timeless call to action, inviting each of us to recognize the sacred in the ordinary and to honor the connections that bind us to one another and to the world. In the practice of rituals, we find not only a reflection of our values but also a means of shaping a more harmonious and meaningful existence.

Chapter 13
Practical Wisdom

In Confucian philosophy, **Zhi** (wisdom) is regarded as a dynamic and essential virtue that bridges knowledge and action. It is not merely the accumulation of information but the ability to apply knowledge in ways that benefit both the individual and society. Zhi represents clarity of thought, insight into ethical complexities, and the capacity to make sound decisions that align with moral principles. Within the Confucian framework, wisdom is not an abstract ideal but a practical tool for navigating life's challenges and achieving harmony in all aspects of existence.

Confucius taught that wisdom begins with an earnest commitment to learning and self-cultivation. He declared, "To know what you know and what you do not know, that is true wisdom." This statement underscores the importance of humility in the pursuit of understanding, recognizing that the journey toward wisdom requires both intellectual curiosity and self-awareness. The wise individual is one who constantly seeks to expand their perspective, acknowledging their limitations while striving for growth.

Zhi is deeply intertwined with other Confucian virtues, particularly **Ren** (humanity), **Yi** (justice), and **Li** (ritual propriety). While Ren inspires compassion and Yi provides the moral compass for discerning right from wrong, Zhi offers the practical insight needed to translate these virtues into effective actions. In this way, wisdom serves as the unifying force that integrates ethical principles into everyday decision-making, ensuring that actions are both thoughtful and virtuous.

In Confucian thought, the path to wisdom begins with education. However, education in this context is not limited to formal instruction; it encompasses a lifelong process of learning from texts, experiences, and interactions. The **Analects** repeatedly emphasize the value of study, with Confucius stating, "He who learns but does not think is lost; he who thinks but does not learn is in danger." This balance between study and reflection is key to cultivating Zhi, as it enables individuals to transform theoretical knowledge into practical understanding.

Wisdom also requires the ability to perceive the deeper meaning in everyday situations. Confucius encouraged his disciples to observe the patterns of nature, the dynamics of human relationships, and the lessons of history as sources of insight. He believed that wisdom is not confined to abstract principles but is revealed in the rhythms and realities of life itself. By paying attention to the world around them, individuals can develop a heightened awareness of the interconnectedness of all things, a perspective that informs wise decision-making.

One of the hallmarks of Zhi is the ability to adapt to changing circumstances. Confucius taught that wisdom involves recognizing the uniqueness of each situation and responding with flexibility and creativity. This requires not only a deep understanding of ethical principles but also the capacity to interpret and apply them in context. For example, the appropriate expression of Ren or Yi may vary depending on the specific needs and dynamics of a given moment. Wisdom, therefore, is not static but dynamic, shaped by the interplay between principle and circumstance.

The practical nature of Zhi is evident in its application to leadership and governance. Confucius argued that wisdom is an essential quality for rulers, enabling them to navigate the complexities of statecraft and to make decisions that promote the welfare of their people. He believed that wise leaders act not out of personal ambition but out of a genuine commitment to the common good. "A leader who governs with wisdom and virtue,"

Confucius declared, "inspires trust and loyalty, for their actions reflect both insight and integrity."

In governance, wisdom involves balancing competing interests and priorities, ensuring that policies are both just and effective. It requires the ability to anticipate the consequences of actions, to assess risks and opportunities, and to adapt strategies as circumstances evolve. Confucius emphasized that wisdom in leadership is inseparable from moral character, asserting that only those who act with virtue can make truly wise decisions.

Zhi also plays a crucial role in interpersonal relationships. Confucius taught that wisdom enables individuals to navigate the complexities of human interaction with grace and empathy. A wise person understands the perspectives and needs of others, fostering mutual respect and cooperation. This quality is particularly important in resolving conflicts, as wisdom provides the insight needed to address underlying issues and to seek solutions that promote harmony.

The cultivation of wisdom is a gradual and ongoing process, requiring dedication and practice. Confucius encouraged his disciples to engage in regular self-reflection, examining their thoughts and actions to ensure that they align with ethical principles. This practice of introspection not only deepens understanding but also fosters a sense of accountability, reinforcing the connection between wisdom and virtue.

Later Confucian thinkers expanded on the concept of Zhi, exploring its philosophical and practical dimensions. **Mencius**, for instance, emphasized the role of wisdom in recognizing and nurturing the inherent goodness of human nature. He argued that Zhi enables individuals to discern the potential for virtue in themselves and others, guiding them toward ethical growth.

Xunzi, by contrast, highlighted the importance of discipline and external guidance in cultivating wisdom. He believed that human nature requires refinement through education and social structures, asserting that Zhi emerges from the deliberate effort to align one's behavior with moral principles. Despite their differing perspectives, both Mencius and Xunzi affirmed the transformative power of wisdom as a force for personal and social harmony.

In the modern world, the principles of Zhi offer valuable insights for addressing contemporary challenges. Whether in leadership, education, or personal development, wisdom provides a framework for making decisions that are thoughtful, ethical, and effective. Its emphasis on balance, adaptability, and foresight resonates with the complexities of modern life, offering a path toward greater understanding and harmony.

In professional settings, Zhi encourages individuals to approach problems with clarity and creativity, considering both immediate needs and long-term implications. In interpersonal relationships, it fosters empathy and mutual respect, enabling individuals to build trust and resolve conflicts. In governance, it inspires leaders to act with integrity and vision, prioritizing the welfare of their communities over personal gain.

Ultimately, Zhi is more than a virtue; it is a way of engaging with the world, a commitment to seeking truth and acting with purpose. Confucianism teaches that wisdom is not an unattainable ideal but a quality that can be cultivated by anyone willing to learn, reflect, and grow. Through the practice of Zhi, individuals can transcend their limitations, contributing to the creation of a more just and compassionate society.

Confucius's teachings on wisdom remain a timeless call to action, challenging each of us to think deeply, act ethically, and strive for a life guided by insight and understanding. In the cultivation of Zhi, we find not only the tools for navigating life's complexities but also the inspiration to create a legacy of wisdom and virtue for future generations.

Chapter 14
Mutual Trust

In the Confucian framework, **Xin** (trustworthiness or integrity) serves as the foundation of all human relationships, both personal and societal. It is the virtue that ensures consistency between one's words and actions, fostering reliability, respect, and mutual understanding. Xin is not merely about keeping promises or honoring commitments; it is about cultivating a moral character that inspires confidence and strengthens the bonds of trust within families, communities, and nations.

Confucius regarded Xin as indispensable for the cultivation of virtue and the maintenance of harmony. He stated, "Without trust, words cannot inspire action, and relationships cannot endure." This insight reveals that trustworthiness is not just a personal quality but a social necessity, underpinning the stability of both interpersonal connections and broader societal structures. Xin ensures that individuals and institutions act with integrity, providing the assurance needed for cooperative and ethical interactions.

The essence of Xin lies in the alignment of thought, speech, and action. A person with Xin does not make empty promises or speak carelessly; their words carry weight because they are backed by consistent and honorable conduct. This reliability earns the respect of others, creating a foundation for lasting relationships and effective collaboration. For Confucius, a society without trust is like a structure without a foundation—fragile, unstable, and doomed to collapse.

In the context of family, Xin begins with the fulfillment of one's responsibilities and the honoring of commitments to loved ones. Confucian thought emphasizes that trustworthiness within the family is the first step toward cultivating trust in society at large. When family members act with Xin, they create an environment of mutual respect and support, fostering harmony and strengthening the moral fabric of the household.

Confucius also recognized the critical role of Xin in governance. He taught that a ruler must earn the trust of their people by demonstrating honesty, fairness, and consistency. Without trust, even the most elaborate laws and policies will fail to inspire loyalty or cooperation. "If a ruler cannot be trusted," Confucius warned, "the people will have no foundation upon which to act." This teaching highlights the reciprocal nature of trust, which must be nurtured through virtuous leadership and ethical behavior.

The concept of Xin extends beyond individual relationships to encompass the trust that binds communities and societies. In commerce, trustworthiness ensures fair dealings and fosters economic stability. In diplomacy, it lays the groundwork for peaceful cooperation and mutual respect between nations. In all these contexts, Xin serves as a unifying force, enabling individuals and groups to work together toward common goals.

The cultivation of Xin requires both personal discipline and a commitment to ethical principles. Confucius emphasized that trustworthiness is not an inherent trait but a quality that must be developed through conscious effort. This involves not only fulfilling one's promises but also acting with transparency and accountability. By consistently aligning their actions with their words, individuals demonstrate the reliability that builds trust over time.

Xin is closely linked to other Confucian virtues, such as **Ren** (humanity) and **Yi** (justice). While Ren inspires compassion and Yi ensures fairness, Xin provides the credibility needed to sustain ethical relationships. Together, these virtues create a moral framework that promotes both individual integrity and collective harmony. Confucius taught that a person who embodies

Xin is one who upholds their commitments with sincerity and acts in accordance with their moral convictions.

One of the most striking aspects of Xin is its transformative power. Trustworthiness not only strengthens relationships but also elevates the moral character of the individual. Confucius believed that by practicing Xin, individuals develop a sense of self-respect and inner peace, knowing that their actions align with their values. This inner harmony, in turn, radiates outward, inspiring trust and respect from others.

Historical examples from Confucian tradition illustrate the profound impact of Xin. Stories of virtuous rulers, such as Emperor Yao and Emperor Shun, emphasize their unwavering commitment to honesty and integrity. These leaders earned the trust of their people through consistent and ethical governance, setting a standard of Xin that became a model for future generations. Their legacy demonstrates that trustworthiness is not only a personal virtue but a foundation for effective and just leadership.

The concept of Xin also extends to the realm of education. Confucius taught that teachers and mentors must embody trustworthiness to inspire their students. A teacher who acts with integrity not only imparts knowledge but also serves as a moral exemplar, instilling the value of Xin in their pupils. This emphasis on trustworthiness in education highlights its role in shaping ethical leaders and responsible citizens.

In the modern world, the principles of Xin are as relevant as ever. In an era marked by rapid change and increasing complexity, trustworthiness provides a foundation for stability and cooperation. Whether in business, politics, or personal relationships, the practice of Xin fosters the mutual confidence needed to navigate challenges and build meaningful connections.

In professional settings, Xin encourages ethical conduct and accountability. Organizations that prioritize trustworthiness earn the loyalty of their employees and customers, creating a culture of reliability and respect. Similarly, leaders who act with integrity inspire trust among their teams, fostering collaboration and innovation. The presence of Xin in professional environments ensures that decisions are guided by principles rather than short-term gains, contributing to long-term success.

In interpersonal relationships, Xin is the cornerstone of mutual respect and understanding. Trustworthiness enables individuals to communicate openly, resolve conflicts, and support one another through challenges. By practicing Xin, individuals cultivate relationships that are not only stable but also deeply fulfilling.

Despite its importance, the practice of Xin is not without challenges. In a world where deception and self-interest often prevail, maintaining trustworthiness requires courage and resilience. Confucius acknowledged these difficulties but insisted that the pursuit of Xin is always worthwhile. He believed that trustworthiness is a reflection of one's moral character and that its cultivation leads to a life of greater meaning and purpose.

The Confucian emphasis on Xin offers a powerful reminder of the value of integrity in both personal and collective life. It challenges individuals to act with sincerity, to honor their commitments, and to prioritize the well-being of others. Through the practice of Xin, individuals contribute to the creation of a more trustworthy and harmonious world.

Ultimately, Xin is not just a virtue but a way of being—a commitment to living with integrity and inspiring confidence in others. Confucianism teaches that trustworthiness is the foundation of all ethical relationships, a quality that unites individuals, families, and societies in their shared pursuit of harmony and virtue. By cultivating Xin, we affirm the enduring power of trust to transform our lives and the world around us.

In the words of Confucius: "He who is not trustworthy will find it hard to stand." This timeless teaching reminds us that trustworthiness is not merely a personal quality but a pillar of all human interaction. In practicing Xin, we honor this legacy, building a foundation of integrity and trust that endures across generations.

Chapter 15
Universal Harmony

Confucian philosophy elevates the concept of **He** (harmony) as the ideal that permeates all aspects of human existence, from personal conduct to family relationships, societal interactions, and the natural world. Harmony is not merely the absence of conflict but the presence of balance, cooperation, and mutual flourishing. It represents the dynamic equilibrium that arises when diverse elements coexist in alignment with moral principles and universal order.

For Confucius, harmony was not a passive state but an active pursuit, requiring effort, understanding, and the cultivation of virtue. He declared, "Harmony is the most precious thing." This teaching underscores the centrality of He in Confucian thought, portraying it as the ultimate goal of both individual and collective life. Harmony is the thread that binds the Confucian virtues together, ensuring that their practice leads to unity and balance rather than discord.

At the personal level, He begins with the cultivation of inner harmony. Confucius emphasized the importance of aligning one's thoughts, emotions, and actions with ethical principles. This alignment requires self-discipline, reflection, and the practice of virtues such as **Ren** (humanity), **Yi** (justice), and **Li** (ritual propriety). By achieving harmony within themselves, individuals create a foundation for harmonious relationships with others.

Harmony within the family is a cornerstone of Confucian ethics. The family is viewed as a microcosm of society, where the principles of respect, responsibility, and mutual care are first learned and practiced. Confucius taught that familial harmony begins with **Xiao** (filial piety), the respect and devotion that children show to their parents. This virtue fosters a sense of gratitude and interconnectedness, creating an environment where each family member fulfills their role with sincerity and compassion.

Beyond the family, He extends to social interactions, shaping the way individuals engage with their communities and society at large. Confucius believed that harmony arises when individuals fulfill their roles and responsibilities with integrity and respect for others. This requires not only adherence to social norms but also a commitment to fairness, empathy, and the common good. In this way, He serves as both a personal and collective aspiration, guiding behavior at every level of society.

One of the unique aspects of Confucian harmony is its embrace of diversity. He does not seek to eliminate differences but to integrate them into a cohesive whole. Confucius observed, "The gentleman seeks harmony, not sameness." This teaching highlights the importance of valuing different perspectives, talents, and experiences while working toward a shared purpose. Harmony is achieved not by erasing individuality but by fostering unity through mutual understanding and cooperation.

In governance, He is both a guiding principle and a measure of success. Confucius envisioned a society where rulers governed with virtue and wisdom, creating conditions for harmony among their subjects. He argued that the role of a leader is not to impose order through force but to inspire unity through moral example. "When the ruler is just," Confucius taught, "harmony prevails without the need for commands." This reflects the Confucian belief that harmony is a natural outcome of virtuous leadership.

The pursuit of harmony in governance also requires balancing the needs and interests of different groups. Confucius emphasized the importance of justice and fairness in creating a harmonious society, teaching that policies must promote the welfare of all citizens rather than favoring a select few. This commitment to equity ensures that harmony is not superficial but deeply rooted in ethical principles.

The concept of He also extends to the natural world, reflecting the Confucian view of humanity's interconnectedness with the cosmos. Confucius taught that human actions should align with the rhythms and patterns of nature, fostering a sense of balance and sustainability. This perspective encourages respect for the environment and a recognition of humanity's responsibility to preserve the harmony of the natural world.

The practice of He requires not only individual effort but also collective participation. Harmony is not achieved in isolation but through relationships, dialogue, and cooperation. Confucius emphasized the importance of communication in resolving conflicts and building understanding, teaching that harmony arises when individuals listen to and learn from one another. This collaborative approach reflects the Confucian ideal of a society where all members contribute to the common good.

Historical examples illustrate the transformative power of He in fostering unity and progress. During the early Han dynasty, for instance, Emperor Wen promoted policies based on Confucian principles, creating a period of stability and prosperity known as the **Rule of Wen and Jing**. By prioritizing harmony in governance and encouraging moral cultivation among officials and citizens, the emperor demonstrated how He can serve as a foundation for effective leadership and social cohesion.

The relevance of He extends beyond its historical context, offering valuable insights for contemporary challenges. In an increasingly interconnected and diverse world, the pursuit of harmony provides a framework for addressing conflicts, fostering inclusion, and promoting sustainable development. The principles of He remind us that unity is not about uniformity but about finding balance amid diversity, creating spaces where all voices are valued, and all perspectives are considered.

In personal relationships, He encourages individuals to prioritize understanding and cooperation over competition and division. By practicing empathy, patience, and respect, individuals can build stronger and more meaningful connections. In professional settings, He inspires collaboration and teamwork, creating environments where diverse talents and perspectives contribute to shared success.

In global relations, the principles of He offer a vision for peaceful coexistence among nations. Confucian harmony emphasizes dialogue and mutual respect as the foundation for resolving disputes and building partnerships. This approach aligns with the growing recognition of the need for collaborative solutions to global issues such as climate change, inequality, and conflict.

Despite its emphasis on unity, the pursuit of He is not without challenges. Confucius acknowledged that achieving harmony requires effort, wisdom, and moral courage. It involves navigating differences, resolving tensions, and addressing injustices with integrity and compassion. Yet, he believed that the pursuit of harmony is always worthwhile, offering a path toward greater understanding and collective flourishing.

Ultimately, He is more than a virtue; it is a vision for a life and a world guided by balance, respect, and interconnectedness. It calls individuals to rise above self-interest, to embrace diversity, and to work toward the common good. By cultivating harmony within themselves and their communities, individuals contribute to the creation of a just and compassionate society, one where all can thrive.

Confucius's teachings on He remain a timeless guide, reminding us that harmony is not a static state but an ongoing journey. It is a call to action, inviting each of us to align our actions with our values, to seek unity amid diversity, and to build a world where balance and cooperation prevail. Through the pursuit of He, we honor the Confucian legacy, creating a foundation for lasting peace and prosperity.

Chapter 16
Natural Order

The concept of **Tian** (Heaven) occupies a central place in Confucian thought, representing the universal moral order that governs both the cosmos and human life. For Confucius, Tian was not merely a distant divine entity but an active force that shaped ethical principles and provided a framework for human conduct. He believed that living in alignment with this natural order was essential for achieving personal virtue, social harmony, and cosmic balance.

Confucius described Tian as the source of moral authority and the ultimate standard of justice. In his teachings, he often referred to the **Mandate of Heaven** (Tianming), a principle that conferred legitimacy on rulers who governed with virtue and wisdom. This mandate was not an entitlement but a conditional responsibility; it could be withdrawn if a ruler failed to uphold ethical governance. In this way, Tian served as both a guiding principle and a reminder of the accountability that comes with power.

The idea of Tian as a moral force is deeply rooted in ancient Chinese traditions, which viewed the cosmos as an interconnected system governed by harmony and balance. Confucius inherited this worldview and expanded its ethical dimensions, teaching that human actions must reflect and uphold the natural order. He believed that by aligning their behavior with the principles of Tian, individuals could contribute to the stability and prosperity of their families, communities, and societies.

At the individual level, living in accordance with Tian begins with **self-cultivation**. Confucius taught that each person has a moral duty to refine their character and to act with integrity, humility, and compassion. This process of self-cultivation is not only a personal endeavor but also a means of harmonizing with the larger cosmic order. By embodying virtues such as **Ren** (humanity), **Yi** (justice), and **Li** (ritual propriety), individuals become agents of Tian, reflecting its moral authority in their daily lives.

Tian also plays a central role in the Confucian vision of governance. A ruler who aligns with the principles of Tian leads with virtue and sets an example for their subjects. Confucius emphasized that such a ruler acts as a mediator between Heaven and Earth, ensuring that their policies and actions promote justice, harmony, and the common good. He declared, "He who governs with virtue may be compared to the polestar, which remains in its place while all the stars turn toward it."

The Mandate of Heaven was a particularly powerful concept in Confucian governance, as it introduced the idea of moral accountability for rulers. Unlike divine-right theories that granted unconditional authority, the Mandate of Heaven required rulers to earn their legitimacy through ethical leadership. If a ruler acted selfishly, abused their power, or failed to meet the needs of their people, they risked losing the mandate, often manifesting as political instability or natural disasters.

This perspective reinforced the reciprocal nature of leadership in Confucian thought. Just as subjects were expected to show loyalty and respect to their rulers, rulers were obligated to act in the best interests of their people. The alignment of governance with Tian ensured that power was exercised not for personal gain but for the welfare of the entire society.

Tian's influence extends beyond governance to encompass the natural world. Confucianism teaches that humanity is not separate from nature but is deeply interconnected with it. Tian represents the cosmic order that binds all elements of existence, from the movements of the stars to the rhythms of the seasons. Confucius emphasized the importance of respecting and preserving this order, teaching that environmental stewardship is a moral responsibility.

This holistic view of Tian encourages a sense of balance and sustainability in human interactions with nature. By recognizing their place within the larger cosmic system, individuals and societies are called to act with mindfulness and restraint, ensuring that their actions do not disrupt the harmony of the natural world. This perspective resonates with contemporary concerns about environmental sustainability, offering timeless principles for addressing modern ecological challenges.

Tian also serves as a source of inspiration and guidance for personal growth. Confucius often spoke of the **Way of Heaven** (Tian Dao) as a path that individuals could follow to achieve moral excellence and fulfillment. This path is not rigid or prescriptive but requires wisdom, discernment, and a deep understanding of ethical principles. By seeking alignment with Tian, individuals cultivate a sense of purpose and direction, finding meaning in their actions and contributions.

In addition to its moral and cosmic dimensions, Tian carries a profound spiritual significance. While Confucius did not focus on metaphysical or theological explanations, he acknowledged the mystery and majesty of Heaven as a force beyond human comprehension. He stated, "Heaven does not speak, yet the four seasons run their course, and all things are produced." This perspective reflects a reverence for the natural order and an acceptance of its inherent complexity.

Later Confucian thinkers, such as **Mencius** and **Xunzi**, offered differing interpretations of Tian. Mencius emphasized the benevolent and nurturing aspects of Heaven, portraying it as a moral force that supports human goodness. He argued that the principles of Tian are reflected in human nature, encouraging individuals to cultivate their innate virtues.

Xunzi, on the other hand, took a more pragmatic view, emphasizing the need for human effort and social institutions to align with the natural order. While he acknowledged the authority of Tian, he focused on the practical means by which individuals and societies could achieve harmony. Despite their differing perspectives, both thinkers affirmed the centrality of Tian in Confucian ethics, highlighting its role as a source of moral guidance and cosmic balance.

The relevance of Tian in contemporary life lies in its emphasis on interconnectedness, accountability, and ethical leadership. In a world marked by social fragmentation and environmental challenges, the principles of Tian offer a framework for fostering unity and sustainability. By aligning with the natural order, individuals and societies can work toward a future that honors both human dignity and the integrity of the planet.

In governance, the concept of Tian challenges leaders to prioritize the welfare of their people and to act with transparency and compassion. It reminds us that power is not a privilege but a responsibility, one that must be exercised in service of the greater good. In personal life, Tian inspires individuals to cultivate their virtues, to act with integrity, and to seek harmony in their relationships and communities.

The legacy of Tian is one of balance, justice, and reverence for the natural order. It calls each of us to recognize our place within the larger cosmic system and to live in alignment with its principles. By embracing the wisdom of Tian, we honor the Confucian vision of a life guided by virtue, harmony, and the pursuit of the common good.

In the words of Confucius: "He who understands Heaven's mandate will not complain against Heaven." This teaching reminds us that Tian is not only a moral standard but also a source of resilience and inspiration. Through our alignment with the natural order, we find not only guidance but also the strength to navigate life's challenges, creating a legacy of harmony and virtue that endures across generations.

Chapter 17
Social Hierarchy

In Confucian thought, the concept of hierarchy is not merely a system of social organization but a reflection of the natural order and a foundation for societal harmony. It is rooted in the belief that every individual occupies a unique position within a web of relationships, each with distinct roles and responsibilities. This structured approach to human interaction, known as **Lunli** (ethical relationships), emphasizes the importance of order, respect, and mutual obligation in maintaining balance and stability in society.

Confucius taught that social hierarchy is not oppressive but purposeful, serving as a guide for ethical behavior and collective well-being. He stated, "Let the ruler be a ruler, the minister a minister, the father a father, and the son a son." This teaching highlights the importance of fulfilling one's role with integrity and dedication, as doing so contributes to the harmony of the whole. The Confucian vision of hierarchy is thus both moral and functional, ensuring that each person's actions align with their responsibilities.

At the heart of Confucian hierarchy are the **Five Relationships (Wu Lun)**, which define the core social bonds: ruler and subject, parent and child, husband and wife, elder sibling and younger sibling, and friend and friend. These relationships are not rigidly hierarchical but emphasize reciprocity and mutual respect. For Confucius, the quality of these interactions determines the moral fabric of society, as harmony in these fundamental relationships extends outward to create a well-ordered community.

The relationship between **ruler and subject** serves as a model for ethical governance. Confucius believed that a ruler's legitimacy depends on their ability to govern with virtue and compassion. In return, subjects are expected to show loyalty and support for their ruler. This reciprocity ensures that power is exercised responsibly and that citizens are treated with fairness and dignity. Confucius stated, "When a ruler loves what is good, the people will also love what is good." This teaching underscores the transformative potential of virtuous leadership, which inspires trust and cooperation throughout society.

In the family, the relationship between **parent and child** is the cornerstone of Confucian hierarchy. It is guided by the principle of **Xiao** (filial piety), which calls for children to honor and care for their parents while parents nurture and guide their children with love and wisdom. Filial piety extends beyond immediate family to include respect for elders and ancestors, reinforcing a sense of continuity and connection across generations. Confucius taught that filial piety is the root of all virtue, as it instills the values of respect, responsibility, and gratitude that underpin harmonious relationships.

The relationship between **husband and wife** reflects the Confucian emphasis on complementary roles within the household. While traditional interpretations often emphasized the authority of the husband and the supportive role of the wife, Confucian thought also highlights the mutual respect and cooperation necessary for a harmonious partnership. By fulfilling their respective responsibilities with care and dedication, both partners contribute to the stability and prosperity of the family.

The dynamic between **elder and younger siblings** represents the importance of hierarchy within the family structure. The elder sibling is expected to act as a role model, demonstrating virtue and responsibility, while the younger sibling shows respect and deference. This relationship reinforces the value of mentorship and the importance of learning from those who have greater experience and wisdom.

The relationship between **friends** is unique among the Five Relationships, as it is based on equality and mutual trust rather than hierarchy. In Confucian thought, friendship provides a space for moral growth and mutual support, as individuals challenge and inspire one another to cultivate virtue. Confucius stated, "When you meet someone better than yourself, turn your thoughts to becoming their equal. When you meet someone not as good as you, look within and examine yourself." This teaching illustrates the role of friendship in fostering self-improvement and moral reflection.

While the Five Relationships provide a framework for ethical interaction, Confucian hierarchy is not static or authoritarian. It is guided by the principle of **Ren** (humanity), which emphasizes compassion, empathy, and the intrinsic value of every individual. Confucius warned against the abuse of power, teaching that true authority is earned through virtue and service rather than coercion or domination. He declared, "He who rules by virtue is like the North Star, which remains in its place while all the stars turn toward it."

Confucian hierarchy also acknowledges the importance of adaptability and context. While roles and responsibilities provide a foundation for ethical behavior, they must be interpreted and applied with wisdom. For example, a ruler who fails to act virtuously forfeits the loyalty of their subjects, just as a parent who neglects their duties loses the moral authority to demand filial piety. This perspective ensures that hierarchy is a means of promoting harmony rather than perpetuating injustice.

The flexibility of Confucian hierarchy is evident in its capacity to evolve in response to changing social and cultural conditions. Over the centuries, Confucian ideals have been reinterpreted and adapted to address new challenges, from the rise of meritocracy to the increasing emphasis on gender equality. These adaptations demonstrate the enduring relevance of Confucian principles, which provide a foundation for ethical interaction while allowing for growth and innovation.

In modern society, the Confucian concept of hierarchy offers valuable insights for navigating relationships and fostering cooperation. In the workplace, for example, Confucian hierarchy encourages leaders to act with integrity and to inspire trust among their teams. By fulfilling their responsibilities with diligence and respect, leaders create an environment where employees feel valued and motivated to contribute their best efforts.

In the family, Confucian hierarchy emphasizes the importance of mutual care and support, reminding individuals of their interconnectedness and shared responsibilities. By honoring their roles within the household, family members create a foundation for harmony and resilience, fostering relationships that endure across generations.

In governance, the Confucian emphasis on virtuous leadership and reciprocal obligation provides a framework for ethical policymaking and public service. Leaders who act with fairness, transparency, and compassion earn the trust of their citizens, creating conditions for stability and progress. Similarly, citizens who engage with their communities and fulfill their civic duties contribute to the collective welfare, embodying the principles of Confucian hierarchy.

Despite its emphasis on order, Confucian hierarchy is ultimately a call to action, challenging individuals to fulfill their roles with virtue and purpose. It reminds us that harmony is not achieved through rigid adherence to rules but through the thoughtful practice of respect, responsibility, and mutual care. By embracing the principles of Confucian hierarchy, we create a society where every individual has the opportunity to thrive and contribute to the common good.

In the words of Confucius: "When everyone fulfills their roles, harmony prevails." This teaching captures the essence of Confucian hierarchy, inviting each of us to recognize our place within the greater whole and to act with integrity, compassion, and dedication. Through the practice of ethical relationships, we honor the legacy of Confucian thought, building a world guided by balance, respect, and shared responsibility.

Chapter 18
Filial Piety

At the core of Confucian ethics lies the principle of **Xiao** (filial piety), the virtue that governs the relationship between children and their parents and extends to all forms of respect for elders and ancestors. Xiao is more than an individual duty; it is the foundation of all moral conduct and the cornerstone of a harmonious society. Confucius taught that filial piety is the root of virtue, a practice that cultivates respect, gratitude, and responsibility, which radiate outward to influence relationships at every level.

Confucius described Xiao as the first step in moral development, stating, "Filial piety and fraternal submission are the roots of all benevolent actions." This teaching highlights the interconnectedness of filial piety with other virtues, such as **Ren** (humanity), **Yi** (justice), and **Li** (ritual propriety). By honoring their parents, individuals learn to embody compassion, fairness, and respect, laying the groundwork for ethical behavior in broader social contexts.

Filial piety begins within the family, where it is expressed through acts of care, obedience, and reverence. Confucian thought emphasizes that children owe their parents not only material support but also emotional warmth and moral respect. This duty extends beyond childhood, continuing throughout life as a reciprocal relationship of love and responsibility. Confucius taught, "In serving one's parents, it is best to follow their wishes while they are alive and to honor their legacy after they are gone."

Xiao also encompasses the care and reverence for ancestors, reflected in the practice of ancestral worship. By performing rituals to honor their forebears, individuals express gratitude for the sacrifices of previous generations and reaffirm their connection to the family lineage. These acts of remembrance are not merely ceremonial but serve as a moral reminder of one's place within the continuum of family and society.

Filial piety is deeply rooted in the Confucian vision of harmony, where the family is regarded as the microcosm of society. Confucius believed that the values learned within the household—respect, loyalty, and mutual care—are the same principles that sustain social order and stability. He declared, "When the family is regulated, the state is well governed; when the state is well governed, the world is at peace." This perspective underscores the transformative power of Xiao, which bridges the private and public spheres.

While filial piety emphasizes obedience and respect, Confucius also recognized the importance of moral discernment within this relationship. He taught that true Xiao involves guiding parents toward virtuous actions and correcting them when they act unjustly. "When parents have faults," Confucius advised, "children should respectfully point them out and gently persuade them to change." This teaching reveals that filial piety is not blind submission but a dynamic and reciprocal process, grounded in mutual care and ethical responsibility.

The practice of Xiao extends beyond individual families to influence the broader community. In Confucian thought, filial piety inspires a sense of responsibility and compassion that shapes one's interactions with others. For example, the respect shown to one's parents naturally leads to the respect of elders and authority figures in society. Similarly, the care given to family members fosters a spirit of generosity and service that benefits the larger community.

Historical examples illustrate the profound impact of Xiao on personal character and social harmony. Stories from Confucian tradition often highlight individuals who demonstrated exceptional filial piety, such as **Zengzi**, a disciple of Confucius known for his unwavering devotion to his parents. Zengzi's acts of care and obedience became models for future generations, embodying the values of loyalty, humility, and selflessness that define Xiao.

Filial piety also played a central role in Confucian governance, shaping the relationship between rulers and their subjects. Confucius envisioned the ruler as a parental figure, responsible for the well-being of the people. In return, citizens were expected to show loyalty and support for their leaders, mirroring the dynamics of filial piety within the family. This analogy reinforced the importance of virtuous leadership, as a ruler who acted with compassion and integrity earned the trust and respect of their subjects.

The concept of Xiao also influenced education, as Confucius emphasized the importance of filial piety in moral instruction. He believed that by learning to honor their parents, students developed the discipline and ethical foundation needed to pursue other virtues. Teachers were expected to serve as role models, embodying the principles of Xiao in their own lives and inspiring their students to do the same.

Despite its traditional roots, the principles of Xiao remain relevant in modern society. In an era marked by rapid change and increasing individualism, filial piety offers a framework for nurturing connection, gratitude, and mutual care within families and communities. By emphasizing the importance of relationships and responsibilities, Xiao challenges the isolation and fragmentation often seen in contemporary life.

In familial relationships, the practice of Xiao fosters stronger bonds and a deeper sense of belonging. By honoring their parents and supporting their needs, individuals create an environment of trust and reciprocity that benefits all members of the household. This commitment to mutual care extends beyond biological families, inspiring acts of kindness and service within diverse communities.

In professional and social settings, the values of Xiao encourage respect for authority, cooperation, and ethical leadership. By applying the principles of filial piety to workplace relationships, individuals cultivate a culture of trust, loyalty, and shared responsibility. Similarly, leaders who embody the spirit of Xiao act with humility and compassion, fostering environments where everyone feels valued and supported.

The challenges of practicing Xiao in the modern world highlight the need for balance and adaptation. While traditional interpretations of filial piety often emphasized obedience, contemporary perspectives recognize the importance of dialogue and mutual respect within family dynamics. By integrating these principles with modern values such as equality and individuality, Xiao can continue to serve as a source of moral guidance and social cohesion.

The Confucian emphasis on Xiao offers a powerful reminder of the interconnectedness of all human relationships. It challenges individuals to look beyond their own needs, to honor the contributions of those who came before them, and to act with compassion and responsibility toward future generations. Through the practice of filial piety, individuals contribute to the creation of a more harmonious and ethical world.

In the words of Confucius: "Filial piety is the foundation of virtue and the root of civilization." This teaching captures the enduring significance of Xiao, inviting each of us to recognize our place within the family and society and to act with integrity, gratitude, and care. By embodying the principles of filial piety, we honor the legacy of Confucian thought, building a foundation for lasting harmony and mutual respect.

Chapter 19
Family Bonds

In Confucianism, the family is more than a social institution; it is the moral foundation upon which all of society is built. Relationships within the family serve as a microcosm of the ethical principles that govern broader human interactions. Central to this understanding are the **Five Cardinal Relationships (Wu Lun)**, with particular emphasis on the familial bonds between parent and child, siblings, and spouses. Confucius regarded these relationships as the starting point for the cultivation of virtue, teaching that harmony in the family radiates outward to create a stable and moral society.

The family, in Confucian thought, is not just a unit of kinship but a space where values such as respect, responsibility, and love are learned and practiced. Confucius stated, "The strength of a nation derives from the integrity of the home." This teaching underscores the belief that the moral health of society depends on the cultivation of ethical relationships within the family. The home becomes the training ground for virtues like **Ren** (humanity), **Li** (ritual propriety), and **Xiao** (filial piety), which prepare individuals for their roles in the wider community.

At the heart of family bonds is the principle of **Xiao**, or filial piety, which governs the relationship between parents and children. As discussed in the previous chapter, Xiao emphasizes respect, care, and obedience toward one's parents, creating a foundation of mutual responsibility. However, Confucianism also stresses that this relationship is reciprocal: parents must provide guidance, love, and moral education, ensuring that their children grow into virtuous and responsible adults.

The bond between siblings is another vital aspect of family life in Confucianism. Elder siblings are expected to act as role models, demonstrating virtue and responsibility, while younger siblings are encouraged to show respect and support. This dynamic fosters a sense of mutual care and cooperation, reinforcing the importance of hierarchy and harmony within the family. Confucius taught that when siblings interact with kindness and respect, they set an example for other relationships, contributing to the overall harmony of society.

The relationship between spouses in Confucian thought is based on complementary roles and mutual respect. While traditional interpretations often emphasized the hierarchical aspects of this relationship, with the husband as the head of the household and the wife in a supportive role, Confucianism also recognizes the importance of partnership and shared responsibility. Confucius emphasized that both spouses must fulfill their duties with sincerity and commitment, working together to create a stable and loving home.

Family bonds are not confined to the present generation; they extend to include ancestors and descendants, reflecting the Confucian emphasis on continuity and connection. Ancestral reverence is a key component of family life, with rituals performed to honor the memory and contributions of forebears. These practices instill a sense of gratitude and responsibility, reminding individuals of their place within a larger lineage. Confucius taught that by remembering their ancestors, individuals cultivate humility and a sense of belonging, which strengthen the bonds of family and society.

In Confucianism, the family is also a site for the practice of **Li**, or ritual propriety. Rituals play a central role in reinforcing family bonds, from daily expressions of respect, such as greetings and gestures of deference, to formal ceremonies like weddings, funerals, and ancestral offerings. These rituals are not merely symbolic; they serve as tangible expressions of love, respect, and unity. Confucius believed that through the practice of rituals, individuals internalize the values that sustain familial and social harmony.

The family's role as a moral institution extends to its influence on governance and society. Confucius argued that the virtues learned within the family—respect for authority, care for others, and responsibility for one's actions—are the same principles that underpin ethical leadership and civic engagement. He stated, "To rule a state, one must first regulate the family." This teaching highlights the interconnectedness of private and public life, suggesting that the cultivation of virtue within the home is a prerequisite for the cultivation of virtue in society.

Despite its emphasis on hierarchy and tradition, Confucianism acknowledges the dynamic nature of family relationships. Confucius recognized that familial roles must be guided by love and moral responsibility rather than rigid authority. He taught that true leadership within the family comes from setting a virtuous example, stating, "The superior man acts with benevolence, and the family follows." This perspective ensures that familial bonds are grounded in mutual care and ethical conduct rather than coercion or domination.

The strength of family bonds is particularly evident in times of adversity. Confucianism teaches that families provide a source of resilience and support, helping individuals navigate challenges and maintain their moral compass. Whether through acts of care for aging parents, guidance for younger siblings, or mutual encouragement between spouses, family members serve as pillars of strength and stability. Confucius viewed these acts of devotion as both a moral duty and a source of personal fulfillment, stating, "In caring for one's family, one finds joy."

The enduring relevance of Confucian family values lies in their ability to address the challenges of modern life. In an era of rapid social change and increasing individualism, the principles of mutual respect, responsibility, and care within families offer a counterbalance to the fragmentation often seen in contemporary society. By prioritizing the cultivation of strong familial bonds, individuals create a foundation for personal growth, social harmony, and collective well-being.

In today's world, Confucian family values can be applied in diverse contexts, from nurturing relationships within nuclear families to fostering connections within extended and chosen families. These principles encourage open communication, mutual support, and shared responsibility, creating environments where all members feel valued and respected. By emphasizing the importance of relationships and responsibilities, Confucianism provides a framework for navigating the complexities of modern family life.

The influence of Confucian family values also extends to professional and social settings. In the workplace, the emphasis on respect, cooperation, and mentorship mirrors the dynamics of familial relationships. Leaders who embody the principles of Confucian family ethics inspire trust and loyalty, fostering a culture of collaboration and mutual care. Similarly, communities that prioritize intergenerational support and shared responsibility reflect the values of familial harmony, creating spaces for connection and growth.

Ultimately, Confucian family bonds are not just about individual relationships but about the creation of a moral and harmonious society. They challenge individuals to look beyond their own needs, to honor their connections with others, and to contribute to the collective good. By cultivating respect, responsibility, and love within the family, individuals lay the foundation for a world guided by compassion and virtue.

In the words of Confucius: "When the family is in harmony, everything prospers." This teaching captures the essence of Confucian family bonds, reminding us of their transformative power to shape individuals, strengthen communities, and sustain civilizations. By embracing the principles of familial respect, care, and unity, we honor the legacy of Confucian thought and create a foundation for enduring harmony and shared prosperity.

Chapter 20
Governmental Relationships

In Confucianism, the relationship between rulers and the governed is not merely a political arrangement but a moral bond rooted in trust, responsibility, and mutual care. Governance, in the Confucian vision, is a deeply ethical endeavor, where the ruler serves as a moral exemplar and the people respond with loyalty and support. This relationship reflects the broader Confucian emphasis on reciprocity and virtue, creating a framework for ethical leadership and societal harmony.

Confucius believed that the legitimacy of a ruler derives not from their power or wealth but from their ability to govern with **Ren** (humanity) and **Yi** (justice). He declared, "To govern is to rectify. If you lead by example, who will dare to be unrighteous?" This teaching underscores the Confucian view that the ruler's character is the foundation of effective governance. A virtuous ruler inspires respect and emulation, fostering a stable and harmonious society.

Central to Confucian political thought is the concept of the **Mandate of Heaven (Tianming)**, a principle that confers authority on rulers who govern with virtue and integrity. The Mandate is conditional, meaning that rulers must continuously demonstrate their commitment to the welfare of the people. If they fail to act justly or neglect their responsibilities, they risk losing the Mandate, often resulting in social upheaval or the rise of a new leader. This idea introduces a sense of moral accountability, ensuring that power is exercised in service of the common good.

The relationship between rulers and the governed is often likened to the familial bond between parents and children. A ruler, like a parent, must act with compassion, fairness, and a deep sense of responsibility. In return, the governed, like children, are expected to show loyalty and respect. This analogy emphasizes the importance of care and reciprocity, suggesting that the ruler's role is not to dominate but to nurture and guide. Confucius stated, "The ruler who loves his people is loved by the people, and the ruler who respects his people is respected by the people."

In Confucian governance, the ruler's primary duty is to ensure the well-being of the people. This includes not only meeting their material needs but also fostering their moral and intellectual development. Confucius taught that a truly virtuous ruler educates their subjects, encouraging them to cultivate their virtues and fulfill their roles within society. This approach reflects the Confucian belief that governance is not merely about maintaining order but about creating conditions for personal and collective flourishing.

The practice of **Li** (ritual propriety) also plays a crucial role in governmental relationships. Rituals, in the Confucian sense, are not only expressions of respect and reverence but also tools for reinforcing ethical conduct and social cohesion. For rulers, observing rituals demonstrates their commitment to moral principles and their alignment with the natural order. Public ceremonies, such as ancestral offerings and seasonal celebrations, serve as reminders of the ruler's responsibility to uphold harmony and balance.

Confucius emphasized the importance of benevolent leadership, arguing that rulers should govern through moral example rather than coercion. He stated, "If you govern the people with laws and punishments, they will avoid punishment but have no sense of shame. If you govern them with virtue and ritual, they will have a sense of shame and reform themselves." This teaching highlights the transformative power of ethical leadership, which inspires voluntary compliance and cultivates a sense of shared responsibility among citizens.

The Confucian vision of governance extends to the structure and function of government itself. Confucius advocated for a meritocratic system, where officials are chosen based on their virtue, wisdom, and ability rather than their birth or social status. He believed that only those who embody the Confucian virtues of Ren, Yi, and Li are qualified to lead, as their moral character ensures that they act in the best interests of the people. This emphasis on merit and virtue laid the foundation for the civil service system that became a hallmark of Confucian governance in later dynasties.

The relationship between rulers and the governed is reciprocal, requiring effort and accountability on both sides. While rulers must act with integrity and compassion, the governed must fulfill their roles as responsible citizens. This includes obeying just laws, contributing to the welfare of the community, and holding leaders accountable when they fail to meet their obligations. Confucius believed that a harmonious society depends on this balance, where both leaders and citizens uphold their ethical responsibilities.

Historical examples illustrate the power of Confucian principles in shaping effective governance. The reign of Emperor Wen of the Han dynasty, for instance, is often cited as a model of Confucian leadership. Emperor Wen prioritized the well-being of his people, implementing policies that reduced taxes, promoted education, and ensured fairness in the legal system. His virtuous conduct earned him the loyalty and admiration of his subjects, creating a period of stability and prosperity known as the "Rule of Wen and Jing."

Confucian principles of governance also address the resolution of conflicts and the restoration of harmony. Confucius taught that leaders must approach disputes with fairness and empathy, seeking solutions that uphold justice while fostering reconciliation. He emphasized the importance of dialogue and mutual understanding, stating, "In a well-governed country, those who are near are happy, and those who are far away are drawn closer." This teaching highlights the role of virtuous leadership in bridging divides and promoting unity.

In the modern world, the principles of Confucian governance offer valuable insights for addressing contemporary challenges. In politics, the emphasis on ethical leadership and accountability provides a counterbalance to corruption and authoritarianism. Leaders who act with integrity and prioritize the welfare of their constituents earn the trust and cooperation needed to address complex issues.

In civic life, the Confucian focus on mutual responsibility encourages active participation and engagement. Citizens who embody the virtues of Ren and Yi contribute to the well-being of their communities, fostering a sense of collective purpose and shared responsibility. Similarly, the emphasis on education and self-cultivation ensures that individuals are equipped to fulfill their roles as informed and ethical members of society.

Despite its ancient origins, the Confucian vision of governance remains relevant in a globalized and interconnected world. Its principles of reciprocity, accountability, and moral leadership provide a framework for addressing the complexities of modern governance, from fostering social cohesion to promoting sustainable development. By aligning their actions with ethical principles, leaders and citizens alike can create conditions for lasting harmony and progress.

Ultimately, the Confucian relationship between rulers and the governed is not about power but about service—service to the people, the community, and the moral order. It challenges leaders to act with wisdom, compassion, and humility, and it calls on citizens to fulfill their roles with respect and responsibility. Through the practice of ethical governance, Confucianism offers a vision of a just and harmonious society, where the bonds between rulers and the governed reflect the values of integrity, care, and mutual trust.

In the words of Confucius: "A ruler who governs with virtue is like the wind, and the people are like grass. When the wind blows, the grass bends." This teaching captures the essence of Confucian governance, reminding us of the profound influence of ethical leadership and the transformative power of mutual responsibility. By embracing these principles, we honor the Confucian legacy and build a foundation for a world guided by justice, harmony, and shared prosperity.

Chapter 21
Virtuous Friendship

Friendship holds a unique place in Confucian philosophy, standing apart from the hierarchical relationships of family or governance. It is a bond rooted in equality, mutual respect, and shared moral aspiration. In Confucian thought, friendships serve not only as sources of personal joy and companionship but also as opportunities for moral development and collective harmony. Confucius regarded virtuous friendships as essential for the cultivation of character, offering a space for individuals to inspire and challenge one another in the pursuit of ethical excellence.

Confucius emphasized that friendship must be grounded in virtue and sincerity, rather than personal gain or superficial connection. He observed, "Do not befriend anyone who is not as good as you." This teaching underscores the belief that friendships should elevate and refine one's moral character, encouraging growth and self-improvement. By choosing companions who embody the virtues of **Ren** (humanity), **Yi** (justice), and **Li** (ritual propriety), individuals create relationships that reinforce their commitment to ethical living.

In Confucianism, friendship is seen as a reciprocal relationship, where both parties contribute to and benefit from the bond. This mutual exchange of support, advice, and encouragement fosters a sense of balance and equality. Unlike familial or governmental relationships, which often involve clear roles and responsibilities, friendships in Confucian thought are partnerships built on shared values and mutual respect. This egalitarian nature of friendship reflects the Confucian ideal of harmony, where diverse perspectives and talents come together in unity.

Confucius often highlighted the role of friendship in moral cultivation, teaching that true friends hold one another accountable for their actions. He stated, "A true friend is one who offers candid advice and correction." This principle emphasizes the importance of honesty and constructive criticism in strengthening character. A virtuous friend is not merely a companion in leisure but a guide who helps illuminate the path of ethical living.

The moral dimension of friendship is further illustrated in Confucius's teachings on loyalty and trust. He believed that friendships thrive when individuals act with integrity and keep their commitments. "When a friend makes a promise, they must fulfill it," he taught, emphasizing the importance of reliability and consistency in building lasting bonds. Trust, in Confucian thought, is not just a practical necessity but a reflection of one's moral character.

Friendship also serves as a bridge between individuals and the broader community. In Confucian philosophy, the virtues cultivated within friendships extend outward, shaping interactions with others and contributing to social harmony. By practicing respect, empathy, and cooperation in their friendships, individuals model these values in their relationships with family, colleagues, and neighbors. This ripple effect underscores the interconnectedness of personal and social ethics in Confucian thought.

Historical examples from Confucian tradition illustrate the transformative power of virtuous friendships. The friendship between **Zilu** and **Yan Hui**, two of Confucius's disciples, exemplifies the ideals of mutual support and shared learning. Zilu, known for his courage and decisiveness, complemented Yan Hui's humility and reflective nature. Together, they inspired one another to pursue greater understanding and virtue, embodying the Confucian principle that friendships should foster moral growth.

The importance of virtuous friendship extends to leadership and governance. Confucius taught that rulers and officials should surround themselves with advisors and companions who possess moral integrity and wisdom. "The superior man seeks friends who will correct him," he stated, highlighting the role of honest and virtuous counsel in effective leadership. This teaching reflects the Confucian belief that ethical relationships are essential not only for personal development but also for the well-being of society.

In contemporary life, the Confucian principles of virtuous friendship offer valuable guidance for navigating relationships in a complex and interconnected world. In personal friendships, these principles encourage individuals to prioritize sincerity, mutual respect, and shared values over superficial connections. By cultivating relationships that inspire moral growth, individuals create bonds that are both meaningful and enduring.

In professional settings, the Confucian emphasis on loyalty, trust, and constructive dialogue fosters a culture of collaboration and mutual support. Colleagues who embody these values contribute to a positive and productive environment, where diverse perspectives are valued and ethical behavior is encouraged. Similarly, leaders who seek advice and feedback from trusted advisors demonstrate humility and a commitment to ethical decision-making.

The relevance of Confucian friendship extends to global relationships, where the principles of respect, empathy, and cooperation provide a framework for fostering understanding and collaboration among nations and cultures. In an increasingly interconnected world, the Confucian ideal of friendship as a partnership based on shared values and mutual benefit offers a vision for building bridges across differences and addressing common challenges.

Despite its emphasis on virtue, Confucian friendship also recognizes the importance of joy and companionship. Confucius celebrated the pleasures of friendship, stating, "Is it not a delight to have friends come from afar?" This teaching reminds us that friendships are not only moral endeavors but also sources of happiness and connection. The balance between ethical aspiration and personal joy is a hallmark of Confucian thought, reflecting its holistic view of human relationships.

The cultivation of virtuous friendships is not without challenges. Confucius acknowledged that maintaining ethical relationships requires effort, patience, and a willingness to confront difficult truths. Yet, he believed that the rewards of such friendships—growth, harmony, and shared purpose—far outweigh the difficulties. "To have a friend who can correct you is a treasure," he taught, emphasizing the transformative power of honest and supportive relationships.

In the Confucian vision, friendships are not static but dynamic, evolving as individuals grow and change. This adaptability reflects the Confucian belief in continuous learning and self-improvement. By remaining open to growth and embracing the lessons that friendships offer, individuals deepen their understanding of themselves and the world around them.

Ultimately, Confucian friendship is a call to action, challenging individuals to build relationships that reflect their highest values and aspirations. It is an invitation to look beyond self-interest, to engage with others in a spirit of mutual respect and shared purpose, and to contribute to the creation of a harmonious and ethical society.

In the words of Confucius: "With friends, one may speak honestly, correct one another's faults, and support one another in virtue." This teaching captures the essence of Confucian friendship, reminding us of its potential to shape character, strengthen communities, and inspire collective flourishing. By embracing the principles of virtuous friendship, we honor the Confucian legacy and create a foundation for meaningful and transformative relationships.

Chapter 22
Mutual Respect

At the heart of Confucian thought lies the principle of **mutual respect**, a virtue that governs all human interactions and sustains the moral fabric of society. Mutual respect, or **Jing**, is the acknowledgment of another's inherent dignity and value, regardless of their position or role. In Confucianism, respect is not limited to hierarchical relationships but extends universally, fostering harmony in personal, familial, social, and political spheres.

Confucius believed that respect is the foundation of all virtues, stating, "Without respect, what is there to distinguish rituals from chaos?" This teaching emphasizes that respect is not merely a polite gesture but a fundamental attitude that shapes ethical behavior and social order. It ensures that interactions are guided by care, consideration, and a recognition of shared humanity.

Mutual respect begins within the family, where it is practiced as the cornerstone of relationships between parents and children, siblings, and spouses. For Confucius, filial piety (**Xiao**) is one of the highest expressions of respect, encompassing acts of care, obedience, and gratitude toward one's parents. Similarly, respect between siblings, characterized by deference and support, reinforces the importance of familial harmony. By cultivating respect at home, individuals learn the values that sustain relationships in the broader community.

In friendships, mutual respect creates a bond of trust and equality, where individuals can engage in honest dialogue and shared growth. Confucius taught, "When friends are true, respect follows naturally." This insight highlights the reciprocal nature of respect, where it is both given and earned through virtuous behavior. Respect in friendships encourages open communication, constructive criticism, and the mutual pursuit of moral excellence.

The principle of mutual respect is also essential in governance, where it shapes the relationship between rulers and the governed. Confucius believed that leaders must demonstrate respect for their subjects by acting with virtue, fairness, and compassion. In return, citizens show respect for their leaders through loyalty and adherence to just laws. This reciprocal respect fosters trust and stability, ensuring that power is exercised responsibly and society functions harmoniously.

Respect in governance is rooted in the Confucian concept of **De** (virtue), which holds that a ruler's authority depends on their moral character. A leader who respects their people earns legitimacy and inspires emulation, creating a culture of ethical behavior. Confucius declared, "When the ruler treats the people with respect, the people respect the law." This teaching underscores the transformative power of respect in fostering civic responsibility and social cohesion.

In addition to its role in personal and political relationships, mutual respect is central to the practice of **Li** (ritual propriety). Rituals, in Confucian thought, are expressions of respect that reinforce social bonds and ethical conduct. Whether through bowing, offering gifts, or observing ceremonies, rituals provide a tangible way to honor others and demonstrate regard for tradition and community. Confucius taught that the spirit of respect underlying rituals is more important than their outward form, stating, "Rituals are empty without sincerity."

Respect also extends to the natural world, reflecting the Confucian belief in the interconnectedness of all life. By showing reverence for nature, individuals cultivate humility and gratitude, recognizing their place within the larger cosmic order. This perspective encourages sustainable practices and a harmonious relationship with the environment, aligning with Confucian ideals of balance and harmony.

The cultivation of mutual respect requires mindfulness and effort, as it challenges individuals to rise above selfishness and prejudice. Confucius acknowledged this difficulty, teaching that respect must be cultivated through **self-cultivation** and reflection. "To respect others, one must first respect oneself," he stated, emphasizing the importance of personal integrity as the foundation for respectful behavior.

Respect for oneself involves living in accordance with Confucian virtues such as **Ren** (humanity) and **Yi** (justice), ensuring that one's actions align with moral principles. By cultivating self-respect, individuals gain the confidence and moral clarity needed to treat others with dignity and fairness. This alignment of personal virtue and interpersonal respect creates a cycle of ethical behavior that benefits both individuals and society.

Confucian thought also recognizes the role of education in fostering mutual respect. Through the study of texts, reflection on ethical principles, and participation in rituals, individuals learn to appreciate the value of others and develop the skills needed to navigate relationships with grace and humility. Confucius believed that education is not merely an intellectual pursuit but a moral endeavor, stating, "Education refines character and reveals the path to respect."

Historical examples illustrate the transformative power of mutual respect in Confucian tradition. The relationship between **Duke Wen of Jin** and his advisor **Jie Zhitui**, for instance, is often cited as a model of respect in governance. Jie Zhitui's loyalty and wisdom earned the deep respect of Duke Wen, who honored his contributions by leading with integrity and fairness. This mutual respect strengthened their bond and inspired trust among the people, exemplifying the Confucian ideal of ethical leadership.

In modern society, the principle of mutual respect offers a framework for addressing challenges such as social division, discrimination, and conflict. By emphasizing the intrinsic value of every individual, Confucian respect challenges systems of inequality and promotes inclusive dialogue. In workplaces, schools, and communities, respect fosters environments where diverse perspectives are valued and collaboration thrives.

In global relations, mutual respect serves as a foundation for peaceful coexistence and cooperation. Confucian principles encourage nations to engage with one another in a spirit of dialogue and reciprocity, seeking common ground while honoring cultural differences. This approach aligns with the Confucian vision of harmony, where respect transcends boundaries to create a more just and compassionate world.

Despite its enduring relevance, the practice of mutual respect requires vigilance and adaptation. Confucius warned against superficial displays of respect, teaching that true regard must come from the heart. "Respect without sincerity is like a vessel without water," he stated, highlighting the importance of authenticity in ethical relationships. This insight challenges individuals and societies to cultivate respect that is genuine, consistent, and rooted in shared values.

Ultimately, mutual respect is both a principle and a practice, guiding individuals to honor the dignity of others while striving for personal and collective harmony. It is a call to action, challenging each of us to recognize the interconnectedness of all life and to act with integrity, compassion, and care.

In the words of Confucius: "Respect yourself, and others will respect you." This teaching captures the essence of mutual respect, reminding us that ethical relationships begin with personal virtue and extend outward to shape the world around us. By embracing this principle, we honor the Confucian legacy and create a foundation for enduring harmony and shared prosperity.

Chapter 23
Social Responsibility

Social responsibility is a cornerstone of Confucian philosophy, woven into the fabric of its ethical framework and collective vision. It reflects the Confucian belief that each individual has a duty to contribute to the welfare of others, fostering harmony within families, communities, and the broader society. Far from being an abstract ideal, social responsibility in Confucian thought is a practical and moral obligation that arises from the interconnectedness of all human relationships.

Confucius emphasized that social responsibility begins with the cultivation of the self. He taught, "The superior man sets his mind on virtue; the inferior man sets his mind on material gain." This distinction highlights the Confucian view that personal morality is the foundation of one's contributions to society. By practicing virtues such as **Ren** (humanity), **Yi** (justice), and **Li** (ritual propriety), individuals develop the character and wisdom needed to fulfill their roles within the community.

The family is the first arena where social responsibility is learned and practiced. Confucius regarded the family as the microcosm of society, where individuals cultivate virtues such as filial piety (**Xiao**), respect, and care. These principles form the moral foundation for interactions beyond the household, shaping one's sense of duty toward others. Confucius taught, "Those who cannot care for their families cannot be trusted to care for the state," emphasizing the importance of personal responsibility as the basis for broader contributions.

Social responsibility in Confucian thought extends to the community, where individuals are encouraged to act with compassion, integrity, and fairness. Confucius stated, "To help others achieve their goals is to fulfill one's own." This teaching underscores the reciprocal nature of social responsibility, where acts of kindness and support benefit both the giver and the recipient. By uplifting others, individuals strengthen the bonds of trust and cooperation that sustain the community.

In governance, the principle of social responsibility takes on a broader dimension, emphasizing the role of leaders in promoting the common good. Confucius believed that rulers and officials must act as moral exemplars, guiding their actions by the welfare of the people. He declared, "The virtuous ruler is like the wind; the people are like grass. When the wind blows, the grass bends." This analogy highlights the transformative power of ethical leadership, which inspires citizens to act with responsibility and care.

The Confucian concept of the **Mandate of Heaven (Tianming)** reinforces the idea that leadership is a moral trust, not a privilege. Rulers are held accountable for their actions and are expected to govern with justice, compassion, and wisdom. If they fail to fulfill their responsibilities, they risk losing the Mandate, a reminder that power must always be exercised in service of the greater good. This principle reflects the Confucian belief that social responsibility is universal, extending from the highest levels of leadership to every individual.

Education plays a vital role in fostering social responsibility, equipping individuals with the knowledge and virtues needed to contribute to society. Confucius taught, "The purpose of learning is to serve others." This perspective aligns education with ethical development, emphasizing the importance of knowledge as a tool for addressing social challenges and improving the lives of others. Through study, reflection, and practice, individuals develop the capacity to act with wisdom and compassion.

Rituals (**Li**) also serve as a means of cultivating social responsibility in Confucian thought. By participating in ceremonies that honor ancestors, community leaders, and shared traditions, individuals reinforce their sense of connection and duty to others. Rituals provide a framework for expressing respect, gratitude, and solidarity, fostering a collective spirit that transcends individual interests.

Historical examples illustrate the profound impact of social responsibility in Confucian tradition. The life of **Mencius**, one of Confucius's most prominent disciples, offers a model of ethical leadership and public service. Mencius emphasized the importance of benevolent governance, advocating policies that addressed the needs of the people, such as equitable land distribution and support for the poor. His teachings reflect the Confucian ideal that social responsibility requires both compassion and action.

In modern society, the Confucian principles of social responsibility provide a framework for addressing contemporary challenges such as inequality, environmental degradation, and social fragmentation. By emphasizing the interconnectedness of all human relationships, Confucianism inspires individuals to take responsibility for the well-being of others and to act in ways that promote harmony and sustainability.

In workplaces and organizations, social responsibility translates into ethical practices, equitable treatment, and a commitment to the common good. Leaders who embody Confucian values create environments where employees feel valued and empowered to contribute their best efforts. Similarly, organizations that prioritize community engagement and sustainability reflect the Confucian ideal of collective responsibility, demonstrating their commitment to the welfare of society.

The principle of social responsibility also has implications for global relations, where it encourages nations to collaborate in addressing shared challenges. Confucianism advocates for a spirit of mutual respect, dialogue, and cooperation, recognizing that the well-being of one nation is intertwined with that of others. This perspective aligns with modern efforts to promote peace, sustainability, and social justice on a global scale.

Despite its emphasis on collective welfare, Confucian social responsibility does not diminish the importance of individual agency. Confucius taught that every person has the capacity to make a positive impact, regardless of their position or circumstances. "Do not underestimate the power of a single act of kindness," he advised, reminding individuals that small actions can create ripples of change. This teaching empowers individuals to take initiative and to recognize the value of their contributions.

The practice of social responsibility requires continuous reflection and effort, as it challenges individuals to balance their own needs with those of others. Confucius acknowledged this complexity, teaching that responsibility must be guided by wisdom and discernment. "In helping others, consider what is just," he stated, emphasizing the importance of aligning actions with ethical principles. This perspective ensures that social responsibility is not merely a reactive impulse but a thoughtful and intentional practice.

Ultimately, Confucian social responsibility is a call to action, inviting individuals to recognize their interconnectedness with others and to act with compassion, integrity, and purpose. It challenges each of us to contribute to the creation of a harmonious and ethical society, where the welfare of all is prioritized over individual gain.

In the words of Confucius: "To take responsibility for oneself is to take responsibility for the world." This teaching captures the essence of social responsibility, reminding us that our actions have the power to shape the lives of others and to influence the course of history. By embracing this principle, we honor the Confucian legacy and create a foundation for enduring harmony and shared prosperity.

Chapter 24
Familial Harmony

In Confucian philosophy, the family is more than a unit of kinship; it is the cornerstone of society, a foundation from which moral virtues radiate outward to shape the social and political realms. Familial harmony, therefore, is not merely a private matter but a collective imperative, one that influences the stability and prosperity of the entire community. Confucius regarded the family as the primary arena for cultivating virtue, teaching that harmonious relationships within the household set the stage for order and balance in the wider world.

At the heart of familial harmony is the principle of **Xiao** (filial piety), which emphasizes respect, care, and devotion between parents and children. Filial piety, however, is not a one-sided duty. In Confucian thought, it is a reciprocal relationship, where parents provide guidance and nurture while children honor and support them. This balance creates an environment of mutual trust and responsibility, fostering a spirit of gratitude and connection. Confucius stated, "The root of all virtue lies in filial piety," underscoring its foundational role in personal and social ethics.

Equally important to familial harmony is the bond between siblings, which is governed by respect and cooperation. Elder siblings are expected to act as role models, while younger siblings show deference and support. Confucius taught that these relationships, rooted in kindness and understanding, serve as a microcosm of broader societal interactions. He observed, "When siblings are harmonious, the family thrives; when the family thrives, the nation prospers." This teaching highlights the interconnectedness of family dynamics with the larger social fabric.

The relationship between spouses also plays a crucial role in fostering familial harmony. In Confucian thought, marriage is not merely a personal union but a partnership that upholds the moral and social order. Spouses are expected to fulfill their roles with sincerity, respect, and a shared commitment to the well-being of the family. While traditional interpretations often emphasized hierarchical roles, Confucian ideals also recognize the importance of mutual care and cooperation. Confucius observed, "The home is built on the foundation of shared virtue," reflecting the belief that harmonious marriages contribute to a stable and ethical household.

Confucian rituals (**Li**) are integral to maintaining familial harmony. Rituals such as ancestral offerings, weddings, and rites of passage reinforce bonds and remind family members of their shared responsibilities. These practices are not merely ceremonial; they serve as expressions of respect and gratitude, connecting individuals to their lineage and to the moral values that guide their actions. Confucius believed that rituals cultivate a sense of unity and purpose, stating, "Through ritual, harmony is preserved."

The role of education within the family further strengthens harmony by fostering mutual understanding and moral growth. Parents, in Confucian thought, are not only caregivers but also teachers, responsible for instilling virtues and guiding their children's development. Confucius emphasized the importance of leading by example, teaching that parents who embody the values of **Ren** (humanity) and **Yi** (justice) inspire their children to do the same. Similarly, children who respect and emulate their parents contribute to a cycle of virtue that sustains the family across generations.

Familial harmony is also tied to the Confucian ideal of balance, where each member fulfills their role in accordance with their abilities and responsibilities. This balance does not imply rigidity but flexibility, as family dynamics evolve over time. For example, as parents age, the roles often reverse, with children taking on caregiving responsibilities. Confucius taught, "Harmony lies in the ability to adapt with grace," emphasizing the importance of responding to changing circumstances with empathy and care.

Historical accounts from Confucian tradition illustrate the profound impact of familial harmony on personal and societal well-being. The story of **Mencius and his mother** is often cited as a model of filial devotion and moral education. Mencius's mother moved their household multiple times to ensure that her son grew up in an environment conducive to learning and virtue. Her dedication exemplifies the Confucian belief that harmonious family relationships are built on mutual sacrifice and shared purpose.

The Confucian emphasis on familial harmony extends beyond the household to influence governance and social order. Confucius taught that the values learned within the family—respect, responsibility, and care—are the same principles that sustain ethical leadership and civic engagement. He declared, "To govern a state, one must first regulate the family." This teaching reflects the belief that harmonious families are the foundation of harmonious societies, where individuals act with integrity and compassion in their public roles.

In contemporary society, the principles of familial harmony remain relevant, offering guidance for navigating the complexities of modern family life. Confucian values encourage open communication, mutual support, and a commitment to shared goals, creating an environment where all members feel valued and connected. These principles can be applied to diverse family structures, from nuclear families to extended and chosen families, demonstrating their adaptability and enduring significance.

The challenges of achieving familial harmony in the modern world highlight the need for balance and intentional effort. Confucius acknowledged that family relationships, like all human interactions, require patience, understanding, and a willingness to learn from one another. He observed, "Harmony is not found in the absence of conflict but in the resolution of differences with respect." This insight encourages families to approach challenges as opportunities for growth and connection.

The influence of familial harmony extends to professional and social settings, where the values cultivated within the family shape one's interactions with others. Respect, responsibility, and empathy, learned at home, become the foundation for ethical behavior in the workplace and the community. Leaders who embody these values create environments where collaboration and trust flourish, reflecting the Confucian ideal of harmony as a collective achievement.

Ultimately, familial harmony is both a personal and social endeavor, rooted in the recognition of shared humanity and mutual care. It challenges individuals to look beyond their own needs, to honor their connections with others, and to contribute to the well-being of the family and society. By fostering harmonious relationships at home, individuals create a ripple effect that extends outward, shaping a more just and compassionate world.

In the words of Confucius: "The family is the root of the nation and the foundation of the world." This teaching captures the essence of familial harmony, reminding us of its transformative power to inspire virtue, strengthen communities, and sustain civilizations. By embracing the principles of respect, care, and unity within the family, we honor the Confucian legacy and create a foundation for enduring harmony and shared prosperity.

Chapter 25
Personal Cultivation

In Confucian philosophy, personal cultivation is the cornerstone of moral development and societal harmony. It is the process by which individuals refine their character, enhance their virtues, and align their actions with ethical principles. Confucius viewed personal cultivation as an ongoing journey, one that requires discipline, reflection, and a commitment to self-improvement. This pursuit is not a solitary endeavor but one that contributes to the well-being of family, community, and the larger social order.

Confucius believed that the cultivation of the self is the foundation for all ethical behavior. He taught, "To put the world in order, we must first put the nation in order; to put the nation in order, we must first put the family in order; to put the family in order, we must first cultivate our personal lives." This teaching reflects the Confucian view that individual virtue is the basis for collective harmony, emphasizing the interconnectedness of personal and societal well-being.

The process of personal cultivation begins with **Ren** (humanity), the central virtue in Confucian thought. Ren embodies compassion, empathy, and a deep sense of care for others. Confucius taught that the practice of Ren requires individuals to treat others as they would wish to be treated, fostering relationships grounded in mutual respect and understanding. By cultivating Ren, individuals develop the moral character necessary to contribute to the harmony of their surroundings.

Another key element of personal cultivation is **Yi** (justice or righteousness), which guides individuals in making ethical decisions. Yi emphasizes the importance of acting with integrity, prioritizing what is morally right over personal gain. Confucius declared, "The superior man acts from a sense of justice, not from a desire for reward." This principle challenges individuals to align their actions with their values, demonstrating a commitment to ethical conduct even in difficult circumstances.

Li (ritual propriety) also plays a vital role in personal cultivation. Through the practice of rituals, individuals learn to express respect, gratitude, and humility, reinforcing their connection to others and to the moral traditions of their community. Confucius taught that rituals are not mere formalities but opportunities for self-discipline and reflection, stating, "By observing ritual, we cultivate our character and bring harmony to the world."

Self-discipline is a recurring theme in Confucian personal cultivation. Confucius emphasized the importance of mastering one's desires and emotions, teaching that true freedom comes from self-control. He stated, "The superior man is firm in his principles but gentle in his actions." This balance of strength and kindness reflects the Confucian ideal of inner harmony, where individuals align their thoughts, feelings, and behaviors with their moral values.

Education is a critical tool for personal cultivation in Confucian philosophy. Confucius regarded learning as a lifelong endeavor, one that deepens understanding and sharpens judgment. He taught, "The love of learning is the foundation of all virtue." Through study, individuals gain insight into ethical principles and develop the intellectual and emotional capacity to apply them in their lives. The study of classical texts, reflection on one's experiences, and dialogue with others are all pathways to personal growth.

The practice of self-reflection is another essential aspect of personal cultivation. Confucius encouraged individuals to examine their thoughts and actions regularly, asking themselves whether they have fulfilled their responsibilities and acted in accordance with their values. He taught, "Each day, I examine myself on three counts: Have I been faithful in my duties? Have I been honest in my dealings? Have I learned from my mistakes?" This habit of introspection fosters self-awareness and accountability, enabling individuals to identify areas for improvement and commit to positive change.

Personal cultivation also involves developing virtues such as **Xin** (trustworthiness) and **Zhi** (wisdom). Trustworthiness reflects an individual's commitment to honesty and reliability, building the foundation for strong relationships and ethical leadership. Wisdom, on the other hand, involves the ability to discern right from wrong and to act with foresight and understanding. Together, these virtues enhance one's capacity to navigate complex situations with integrity and grace.

The impact of personal cultivation extends beyond the individual to influence family, community, and society. Confucius taught that a virtuous person inspires others through their actions, creating a ripple effect that promotes harmony and justice. He stated, "The superior man seeks to perfect himself so that he may perfect others." This teaching underscores the transformative power of personal cultivation, demonstrating how individual efforts contribute to collective well-being.

Historical examples illustrate the importance of personal cultivation in Confucian tradition. The life of **Yan Hui**, one of Confucius's most devoted disciples, serves as a model of humility, dedication, and moral integrity. Despite his modest circumstances, Yan Hui focused on cultivating his virtues and practicing Ren in his daily interactions. His unwavering commitment to self-improvement earned the respect of Confucius and his peers, exemplifying the Confucian ideal of a life devoted to ethical growth.

In the modern world, the principles of personal cultivation offer valuable guidance for navigating the complexities of contemporary life. Confucian values encourage individuals to prioritize character development over material success, fostering a sense of purpose and fulfillment. By cultivating virtues such as empathy, integrity, and self-discipline, individuals can build stronger relationships, contribute to their communities, and find meaning in their endeavors.

Personal cultivation also has implications for leadership and professional life. Leaders who embody Confucian virtues inspire trust and loyalty, creating environments where collaboration and ethical behavior thrive. In organizations, the practice of self-reflection and continuous learning aligns with modern principles of personal development and emotional intelligence, demonstrating the enduring relevance of Confucian thought.

Despite its emphasis on self-improvement, personal cultivation in Confucian philosophy is not a solitary pursuit. It is deeply relational, grounded in the understanding that one's growth is inseparable from the well-being of others. Confucius taught that the purpose of personal cultivation is not only to achieve individual excellence but to contribute to the greater good, stating, "The superior man perfects his virtue for the benefit of all."

The journey of personal cultivation is lifelong, requiring patience, perseverance, and a willingness to embrace challenges. Confucius acknowledged that perfection is an aspiration rather than an endpoint, teaching that the pursuit of virtue is a continuous process. He observed, "To improve oneself is to walk the path of humanity; to stop is to stray from it." This perspective encourages individuals to remain committed to their growth, recognizing that every step forward contributes to a life of meaning and purpose.

Ultimately, personal cultivation is the foundation of Confucian ethics, a practice that transforms individuals and societies alike. It challenges us to align our actions with our values, to seek wisdom and virtue, and to contribute to the harmony of the world. In the words of Confucius: "The journey of a thousand miles begins with the cultivation of the self." By embracing this principle, we honor the Confucian legacy and create a foundation for enduring harmony and shared prosperity.

Chapter 26
Lifelong Learning

In Confucian thought, the pursuit of knowledge is not confined to academic or intellectual endeavors; it is a lifelong commitment to self-cultivation and moral development. Confucius saw learning as a process that refines character, enhances wisdom, and prepares individuals to contribute meaningfully to society. His teachings on lifelong learning reflect a profound respect for education as the cornerstone of personal and collective growth, emphasizing that learning is not simply a means to an end but a virtue in itself.

Confucius declared, "Is it not a joy to learn and apply what one has learned?" This statement captures the Confucian belief that learning is a dynamic and practical endeavor, deeply connected to the realities of life. For Confucius, knowledge was not static; it was meant to be applied, refined through experience, and shared with others. He encouraged his disciples to approach learning with curiosity, humility, and a sense of purpose, urging them to seek understanding beyond the superficial or utilitarian.

The Confucian approach to learning is grounded in the cultivation of **Zhi** (wisdom), a virtue that encompasses the ability to discern truth, make ethical decisions, and act with foresight. Wisdom, in this context, is not limited to theoretical knowledge but includes practical insight gained through reflection and lived experience. Confucius taught, "To know what you know and to know what you do not know, that is true knowledge." This teaching emphasizes the importance of self-awareness and the acknowledgment of one's limitations as prerequisites for genuine learning.

Confucianism views education as a moral journey, where the ultimate goal is the cultivation of **Ren** (humanity) and other virtues. Learning is not an end in itself but a path to becoming a better person—one who acts with integrity, compassion, and justice. Confucius stated, "The essence of knowledge is to apply it in the service of others." This principle ties education to ethical practice, reinforcing the idea that true learning is inseparable from the pursuit of virtue.

Lifelong learning in Confucianism is characterized by three interrelated practices: study, reflection, and action.

1. **Study**: Confucius emphasized the importance of engaging with classical texts and teachings as sources of wisdom and inspiration. He encouraged his disciples to read widely and critically, seeking knowledge that deepens their understanding of ethical principles and human nature. At the same time, he warned against blind adherence to tradition, teaching that study must be accompanied by independent thought. "Learning without thought is labor lost; thought without learning is perilous," he observed, highlighting the balance between study and discernment.

2. **Reflection**: Reflection is central to the Confucian model of lifelong learning, as it transforms knowledge into wisdom. Confucius believed that introspection allows individuals to evaluate their actions, identify areas for improvement, and align their behavior with their values. He taught, "When walking with others, I observe both their strengths and their faults. From the virtuous, I learn to improve myself; from the flawed, I learn what to avoid." This habit of reflective learning fosters self-awareness and continuous growth.

3. **Action**: For Confucius, the true measure of learning is its application in daily life. Knowledge that remains theoretical or unpracticed has little value in Confucian thought. He declared, "To study and not act upon what you have learned is a betrayal of knowledge." This

teaching underscores the importance of translating understanding into virtuous conduct, demonstrating that learning is most meaningful when it inspires positive change in oneself and others.

The Confucian emphasis on lifelong learning is not limited to formal education or intellectual pursuits. It encompasses the development of practical skills, emotional intelligence, and moral insight. Confucius taught that learning occurs in every aspect of life, from observing nature to engaging with others in dialogue. He believed that every interaction offers an opportunity to learn and grow, stating, "The superior man is open to learning from all."

Historical examples from Confucian tradition illustrate the transformative power of lifelong learning. The life of **Zengzi**, a devoted disciple of Confucius, exemplifies the practice of study, reflection, and action. Zengzi was known for his rigorous self-discipline and commitment to moral growth, often examining his actions to ensure they aligned with Confucian principles. His dedication to learning and virtue earned him the respect of his peers and a lasting legacy as a model of ethical living.

In modern society, the principles of lifelong learning provide a valuable framework for personal and professional development. In a rapidly changing world, the Confucian emphasis on adaptability, critical thinking, and moral reflection offers guidance for navigating complexity and uncertainty. By embracing the Confucian approach to learning, individuals can cultivate the resilience, wisdom, and empathy needed to thrive in diverse and dynamic environments.

The relevance of lifelong learning extends beyond individual growth to influence organizations, communities, and nations. Confucian values encourage institutions to prioritize education, innovation, and ethical leadership, creating cultures of continuous improvement and collective progress. In workplaces, the practice of reflective learning fosters collaboration and creativity, while in communities, it inspires civic engagement and social responsibility.

Despite its emphasis on discipline and effort, the Confucian vision of lifelong learning is infused with joy and fulfillment. Confucius observed, "He who learns with delight never tires of learning." This teaching reminds us that the pursuit of knowledge is not a burden but a source of inspiration and meaning. By approaching learning with curiosity and gratitude, individuals can find satisfaction in the process of growth, regardless of the challenges they face.

Lifelong learning in Confucianism also emphasizes the importance of humility and openness. Confucius warned against arrogance and complacency, teaching that even the wisest individuals have more to learn. He stated, "The superior man is modest in speech but excels in action," highlighting the value of quiet dedication over boastful display. This attitude of humility fosters a willingness to learn from others, regardless of their background or perspective.

Ultimately, the Confucian practice of lifelong learning is a journey of self-discovery and transformation. It challenges individuals to seek wisdom, cultivate virtue, and contribute to the greater good. In the words of Confucius: "The path of learning is endless, but every step forward brings us closer to harmony." By embracing this principle, we honor the Confucian legacy and create a foundation for enduring growth, understanding, and shared prosperity.

Chapter 27
Moral Education

Moral education occupies a central place in Confucian philosophy, forming the backbone of its vision for individual development and societal harmony. Unlike mere instruction in academic subjects or technical skills, moral education seeks to shape the character and ethical sensibilities of individuals, instilling virtues that guide their behavior in personal, familial, and public life. For Confucius, the ultimate purpose of education is not the accumulation of knowledge but the cultivation of virtue, which leads to a life of integrity and contributes to the greater good.

Confucius believed that education begins with moral principles because ethical conduct is the foundation for all human endeavors. He declared, "A man who does not learn virtue will not stand firm," emphasizing that the stability of both individuals and society depends on moral education. This teaching underscores the Confucian view that education is inseparable from ethics, as the development of intellectual abilities must be accompanied by the cultivation of moral character.

The starting point for moral education in Confucianism is the cultivation of **Ren** (humanity), the highest virtue and the guiding principle for all relationships. Ren embodies compassion, empathy, and a commitment to the welfare of others. Confucius taught that the practice of Ren begins with small acts of kindness and gradually expands to include all of humanity. He stated, "The virtuous person begins with loving their family and extends that love to the community and beyond." This progression highlights the interconnectedness of personal virtue and social responsibility.

Moral education also emphasizes the practice of **Li** (ritual propriety), which instills respect, discipline, and a sense of order. Through the observance of rituals—whether familial, social, or civic—individuals learn to express gratitude, honor tradition, and uphold the values that sustain harmony. Confucius believed that rituals are not mere formalities but essential tools for moral development, stating, "Ritual shapes the heart and refines the character."

Yi (justice) is another cornerstone of moral education in Confucian thought. It teaches individuals to act with integrity, prioritizing ethical principles over personal gain or convenience. Confucius described Yi as the ability to discern right from wrong and to act accordingly, even in challenging circumstances. He advised, "The superior man upholds justice even at great personal cost," reflecting the Confucian ideal of moral courage.

The role of teachers in moral education is paramount. Confucius himself exemplified the ideal educator, combining wisdom, patience, and a deep commitment to his students' moral and intellectual growth. He viewed teaching as a relational process, where the teacher inspires, guides, and challenges students to reach their highest potential. He stated, "A good teacher opens the door, but it is the student who must walk through it," emphasizing the collaborative nature of education.

Teachers in Confucian tradition are not only sources of knowledge but also role models who embody the virtues they teach. Confucius believed that students learn as much from observing their teachers' behavior as they do from their lessons. He declared, "The teacher's character is the foundation of their instruction," highlighting the importance of leading by example. This principle extends to parents, elders, and community leaders, who also play a crucial role in moral education through their actions and guidance.

The process of moral education in Confucianism is holistic, integrating study, reflection, and practice.

1. **Study**: Students are encouraged to engage with classical texts, including the **Analects**, **Mencius**, and other Confucian works, which contain timeless lessons on virtue, ethics, and human relationships. These texts serve as sources of wisdom and inspiration, offering insights into the principles that guide moral conduct. Confucius taught, "By studying the past, we understand the present and prepare for the future."
2. **Reflection**: Reflection is central to moral education, as it transforms knowledge into understanding and action. Confucius encouraged students to examine their behavior, evaluate their progress, and identify areas for improvement. He stated, "The superior man reflects on his actions three times a day: Have I been faithful in my duties? Have I acted with integrity? Have I learned from my experiences?" This practice fosters self-awareness and accountability, essential for moral growth.
3. **Practice**: Moral education is incomplete without action. Confucius emphasized that virtues must be applied in daily life, from small interactions to significant decisions. He declared, "Virtue is not something to be spoken of but to be lived," highlighting the importance of consistency and authenticity in ethical conduct. Through practice, individuals internalize moral principles, making them an integral part of their character.

Historical examples from Confucian tradition illustrate the transformative power of moral education. The story of **Yan Hui**, one of Confucius's most virtuous disciples, exemplifies the ideal student who combines humility, diligence, and a commitment to ethical living. Despite facing hardships, Yan Hui focused on cultivating his character and practicing Ren in his interactions with others. His life serves as a testament to the enduring impact of moral education.

Moral education in Confucianism is not limited to children or students; it is a lifelong process that challenges individuals to grow continuously in virtue and wisdom. Confucius taught, "The journey of learning has no end," encouraging people of all ages to remain open to instruction, reflection, and self-improvement. This perspective aligns with the Confucian ideal of lifelong learning, where education is both a personal and social responsibility.

In modern contexts, the principles of Confucian moral education offer valuable guidance for addressing contemporary challenges, such as ethical leadership, social inequality, and cultural fragmentation. By emphasizing values such as empathy, integrity, and respect, Confucian education fosters individuals who are not only skilled but also committed to the well-being of others. These principles can be integrated into schools, workplaces, and communities, creating environments that prioritize ethical development alongside intellectual and professional achievement.

The relevance of moral education extends to global relations, where it provides a framework for fostering mutual understanding and cooperation among diverse cultures. Confucian values encourage dialogue, respect, and a commitment to the common good, offering a vision for addressing shared challenges with wisdom and integrity.

Despite its emphasis on discipline and effort, Confucian moral education is also characterized by joy and fulfillment. Confucius observed, "To learn and to practice what one has learned is a great delight," reminding us that the pursuit of virtue is not a burden but a source of meaning and satisfaction. This teaching inspires individuals to approach moral education with enthusiasm and gratitude, recognizing its transformative potential for themselves and society.

Ultimately, moral education in Confucianism is a path to becoming a better person and creating a better world. It challenges individuals to align their actions with their values, to seek wisdom through study and reflection, and to act with compassion and justice in all their endeavors. In the words of Confucius: "The superior man perfects his virtue for the benefit of all." By embracing this principle, we honor the Confucian legacy and build a foundation for enduring harmony and shared prosperity.

Chapter 28
Practical Knowledge

In Confucian thought, the value of knowledge lies not in its theoretical abstraction but in its application to the real world. Practical knowledge—understanding that informs and guides ethical actions—is integral to the Confucian vision of a harmonious society. Confucius believed that knowledge is only meaningful when it enhances one's character, improves relationships, and contributes to the greater good. He taught, "Knowledge without action is as fruitless as action without knowledge," emphasizing the inseparable link between understanding and doing.

Practical knowledge, or **Zhi**, is more than the accumulation of facts or mastery of skills. It is wisdom in action, the ability to apply ethical principles to specific situations with clarity and discernment. For Confucius, Zhi is one of the essential virtues, alongside Ren (humanity), Yi (justice), and Li (ritual propriety). He observed, "The wise know what is just; the virtuous do what is just," highlighting the transformative power of knowledge when it is grounded in moral purpose.

The cultivation of practical knowledge begins with self-awareness. Confucius taught that individuals must first understand their own strengths, limitations, and motivations before they can act effectively in the world. He stated, "Knowing yourself is the beginning of wisdom," a principle that underscores the importance of introspection and self-cultivation in acquiring practical knowledge. By reflecting on their experiences and aligning their actions with their values, individuals develop the moral clarity needed to navigate life's complexities.

Practical knowledge also requires an understanding of human relationships and social dynamics. Confucius believed that knowledge is most valuable when it enhances harmony in the family, community, and society. He taught, "The superior man seeks to understand others, for in understanding others, he understands the world." This perspective emphasizes empathy, active listening, and the ability to adapt one's behavior to the needs of others.

The Confucian emphasis on practical knowledge is closely tied to the concept of **Li** (ritual propriety). Through the practice of rituals, individuals learn to express respect, gratitude, and care, cultivating habits that foster social harmony. Rituals provide a framework for navigating relationships and resolving conflicts, offering a practical application of ethical principles. Confucius observed, "Through ritual, the heart is refined, and the path to harmony is revealed."

Education is central to the cultivation of practical knowledge. Confucius believed that study must be accompanied by critical thinking and experiential learning. He declared, "Learning without thought is labor lost; thought without learning is perilous," underscoring the importance of integrating knowledge with action. In the Confucian tradition, education is not merely about acquiring information but about developing the capacity to apply wisdom in daily life.

Historical accounts from Confucian tradition illustrate the importance of practical knowledge. The life of **Zilu**, one of Confucius's most dedicated disciples, offers a compelling example. Zilu was known for his courage and initiative, but his impulsive nature often led to challenges. Under Confucius's guidance, Zilu learned to temper his actions with reflection, transforming his zeal into effective leadership. His journey demonstrates the Confucian ideal of balancing boldness with wisdom, ensuring that actions are guided by ethical understanding.

Practical knowledge in Confucian thought is also closely linked to the concept of adaptability. Confucius recognized that the application of ethical principles varies depending on context and circumstances. He taught, "What is appropriate in one situation may be improper in another," encouraging individuals to use discernment and flexibility in their actions. This adaptability reflects the Confucian belief that wisdom is not rigid but responsive, capable of addressing the nuances of human experience.

In the modern world, the principles of practical knowledge offer valuable insights for addressing contemporary challenges. Confucian values encourage individuals to approach problems with empathy, creativity, and a commitment to ethical solutions. In workplaces, schools, and communities, the application of practical knowledge fosters collaboration, innovation, and social cohesion.

Practical knowledge also has implications for leadership and governance. Confucius taught that leaders must possess not only theoretical understanding but also the ability to act decisively and justly. He stated, "The superior leader knows what is right and does it," reflecting the Confucian ideal of ethical leadership. By combining knowledge with action, leaders inspire trust and guide their communities toward harmony and prosperity.

Despite its emphasis on action, Confucian practical knowledge is not impulsive or reactive. It requires careful reflection, consultation with others, and a commitment to learning from mistakes. Confucius observed, "The wise man learns from his errors and grows stronger," highlighting the importance of resilience and adaptability in the pursuit of wisdom. This perspective encourages individuals to view challenges as opportunities for growth and to approach life with a spirit of humility and openness.

Practical knowledge also extends to the natural world, reflecting the Confucian belief in the interconnectedness of all life. By observing and learning from nature, individuals gain insight into patterns of balance, harmony, and renewal. This understanding informs sustainable practices and a respectful relationship with the environment, aligning with the Confucian ideal of living in harmony with the cosmos.

The pursuit of practical knowledge is a lifelong endeavor, requiring discipline, curiosity, and a willingness to engage with the world. Confucius taught, "The path of wisdom is endless, but each step brings clarity and purpose." This teaching reminds us that knowledge is not a destination but a journey, one that enriches our lives and empowers us to contribute to the greater good.

Ultimately, practical knowledge in Confucian philosophy is a call to action, challenging individuals to align their understanding with their values and to act with integrity, compassion, and foresight. It is a dynamic process that transforms both the individual and the world, creating a foundation for enduring harmony and shared prosperity.

In the words of Confucius: "To know and to act are one and the same." By embracing this principle, we honor the Confucian legacy and build a path to a life of meaning, purpose, and ethical excellence.

Chapter 29
Intellectual Development

In Confucian thought, intellectual development is not an isolated pursuit but a vital part of self-cultivation and the quest for moral and social harmony. It reflects the belief that the mind must be nurtured alongside the heart, fostering wisdom, discernment, and the capacity to apply knowledge ethically. Confucius saw intellectual growth as a dynamic process, one that encompasses curiosity, critical thinking, and the integration of knowledge into virtuous action.

Confucius emphasized that intellectual development begins with a love of learning. He observed, "The superior man delights in learning for its own sake," highlighting the intrinsic value of intellectual pursuits. For Confucius, learning was not merely a means to achieve material success or social status; it was a lifelong journey of self-improvement and enlightenment. This perspective elevates intellectual development beyond academic achievement, framing it as a moral and spiritual endeavor.

Central to Confucian intellectual development is the cultivation of **Zhi** (wisdom). Zhi involves the ability to think critically, make ethical judgments, and respond to complex situations with clarity and foresight. Confucius taught, "Wisdom lies in knowing what is right and acting upon it," underscoring the importance of aligning intellectual understanding with ethical principles. This integration of thought and action reflects the Confucian belief that knowledge must serve a higher purpose.

The process of intellectual development in Confucianism is guided by three interrelated practices: inquiry, reflection, and application.

1. **Inquiry**: Inquiry involves the active pursuit of knowledge through study, observation, and dialogue. Confucius encouraged his disciples to seek understanding with curiosity and openness, exploring diverse perspectives and engaging with classical texts. He declared, "To ask questions is to seek wisdom," emphasizing the importance of intellectual curiosity in uncovering truth. At the same time, Confucius warned against superficial learning, teaching that knowledge must be pursued with depth and sincerity.
2. **Reflection**: Reflection transforms information into insight, allowing individuals to evaluate their understanding and its implications. Confucius believed that reflection fosters self-awareness and critical thinking, enabling individuals to refine their beliefs and actions. He stated, "To study and not reflect is to labor in vain; to reflect and not study is dangerous," highlighting the balance between intellectual rigor and thoughtful contemplation.
3. **Application**: Application is the culmination of intellectual development, where knowledge is translated into virtuous action. Confucius taught that intellectual growth is incomplete without practice, stating, "Learning is of no use unless it is applied." This principle ties intellectual pursuits to ethical behavior, ensuring that understanding is directed toward the betterment of oneself and society.

Confucian intellectual development also emphasizes the study of classical texts, which serve as sources of wisdom and inspiration. Works such as the **Analects**, **Mencius**, and the **Book of Changes** offer timeless lessons on ethics, governance, and human relationships. Confucius regarded these texts as essential tools for cultivating wisdom, teaching that they provide both practical guidance and a deeper understanding of the moral order. He observed, "To study the classics is to connect with the wisdom of the ages."

The role of mentorship in intellectual development is another key aspect of Confucian thought. Confucius himself was a dedicated teacher, guiding his disciples with patience and insight. He believed that learning is most effective when it occurs in the context of a supportive relationship, where mentors inspire, challenge, and nurture their students. He stated, "The best teacher is one who encourages the student to find their own path." This relational approach to education fosters both intellectual growth and moral development.

Historical examples from Confucian tradition illustrate the transformative power of intellectual development. The life of **Mencius**, often regarded as the "Second Sage" of Confucianism, exemplifies the pursuit of wisdom through inquiry, reflection, and application. Mencius expanded upon Confucius's teachings, exploring complex ethical questions and advocating for just governance. His intellectual contributions enriched Confucian thought and demonstrated the enduring relevance of its principles in addressing societal challenges.

In modern contexts, the Confucian emphasis on intellectual development offers valuable insights for education, leadership, and personal growth. Confucian values encourage individuals to approach learning with curiosity, discipline, and a commitment to ethical application. In schools and universities, these principles inspire students to see education as a journey of self-cultivation rather than a means to an end.

The relevance of intellectual development extends to professional and civic life, where critical thinking, adaptability, and ethical decision-making are essential. Confucian teachings on intellectual growth encourage leaders to engage with diverse perspectives, seek innovative solutions, and act with integrity. By fostering a culture of continuous learning, organizations and communities can address challenges with wisdom and resilience.

Despite its emphasis on discipline, Confucian intellectual development is also characterized by joy and fulfillment. Confucius observed, "To learn and to practice what one has learned is a great delight," reminding us that the pursuit of knowledge enriches both the mind and the spirit. This teaching inspires individuals to approach intellectual growth with enthusiasm and gratitude, recognizing its transformative potential.

The Confucian ideal of intellectual development is not confined to formal education or academic achievements. It encompasses all aspects of life, from observing nature to engaging in meaningful conversations. Confucius taught that every experience offers an opportunity to learn, stating, "The superior man learns from all he encounters." This perspective encourages individuals to remain open to new ideas and to see learning as a continuous process.

Ultimately, intellectual development in Confucian philosophy is a path to wisdom, virtue, and harmony. It challenges individuals to seek understanding, to reflect on their values, and to act with integrity in all their endeavors. In the words of Confucius: "The journey of learning has no end, but each step forward brings us closer to the truth." By embracing this principle, we honor the Confucian legacy and create a foundation for enduring growth, understanding, and shared prosperity.

Chapter 30
Integral Formation

In Confucian philosophy, the concept of integral formation encompasses the development of an individual in all dimensions—moral, intellectual, spiritual, and social. This holistic approach aims to create a balanced and harmonious person, one who embodies virtue and wisdom while fulfilling their responsibilities within the family, community, and society. For Confucius, the true measure of a person lies not in isolated achievements but in their ability to integrate these elements into a life of purpose and harmony.

Confucius viewed integral formation as a dynamic and lifelong process, one that begins with self-cultivation and extends outward to influence others. He taught, "To bring order to the world, one must first perfect oneself," emphasizing the interconnectedness of personal growth and social harmony. This principle underscores the Confucian belief that individual development is the foundation for collective well-being.

At the heart of integral formation is the cultivation of **Ren** (humanity), the virtue that embodies compassion, empathy, and a commitment to the welfare of others. Ren serves as the moral compass guiding all aspects of a person's life, ensuring that their actions are rooted in kindness and integrity. Confucius described Ren as the essence of being fully human, stating, "The virtuous person acts with humanity in every circumstance." This teaching reflects the central role of Ren in shaping a life of harmony and balance.

Another essential element of integral formation is the practice of **Yi** (justice), which instills a sense of righteousness and fairness in one's decisions. Yi guides individuals to act with integrity, even in challenging situations, ensuring that their choices align with ethical principles. Confucius taught, "The superior man upholds justice, not for gain but for the sake of virtue," highlighting the importance of prioritizing moral values over personal advantage.

The integration of **Li** (ritual propriety) further strengthens the Confucian vision of holistic development. Through the observance of rituals, individuals learn discipline, respect, and a sense of connection to tradition and community. Rituals serve as practical expressions of ethical values, reinforcing the bonds that unite people and fostering a spirit of gratitude and reverence. Confucius stated, "Through ritual, harmony is achieved within the self and extended to the world."

Integral formation also encompasses intellectual development, encouraging individuals to cultivate **Zhi** (wisdom) through study, reflection, and practical application. Wisdom in Confucian thought is not merely intellectual but deeply connected to ethical insight and the ability to navigate life's complexities with clarity and foresight. Confucius declared, "The wise seek understanding not for its own sake but to act with purpose," emphasizing the practical and moral dimensions of intellectual growth.

The Confucian approach to integral formation also includes the development of spiritual awareness. While Confucianism is not a religion in the conventional sense, it emphasizes a profound respect for the natural and cosmic order, often referred to as **Tian** (Heaven). Confucius taught that aligning oneself with the principles of Tian fosters a sense of purpose and harmony, enabling individuals to live in accordance with the greater moral order. He observed, "The virtuous person harmonizes with Heaven and Earth, finding their rightful place within the cosmos."

The process of integral formation is not a solitary endeavor but one that unfolds in the context of relationships. Confucius emphasized the importance of family as the primary arena for moral and personal development, teaching that the virtues cultivated within the family—respect, care, and responsibility—serve as the foundation for all other relationships. He stated, "The family is the root of virtue; from it, all goodness grows." This perspective highlights the role of family dynamics in shaping a well-rounded and harmonious individual.

Education plays a central role in integral formation, serving as the means by which individuals refine their character and expand their understanding. Confucius believed that education should address all aspects of the self, blending moral instruction with intellectual and practical learning. He observed, "Education transforms the raw material of humanity into the finished work of virtue," reflecting the transformative potential of a well-rounded education.

Historical examples from Confucian tradition illustrate the power of integral formation. The life of **Zengzi**, a devoted disciple of Confucius, serves as a model of balanced development. Known for his deep moral integrity, intellectual rigor, and commitment to family and community, Zengzi exemplified the Confucian ideal of a harmonious and virtuous life. His legacy continues to inspire those who seek to integrate all dimensions of their being into a unified whole.

In contemporary society, the principles of integral formation offer valuable insights for addressing the challenges of fragmentation and imbalance. The Confucian emphasis on harmony, self-cultivation, and relational responsibility provides a framework for navigating the complexities of modern life. By fostering holistic development, individuals can achieve greater resilience, adaptability, and fulfillment, contributing to the well-being of their communities and the world.

Integral formation also has implications for leadership and governance. Confucius taught that leaders must embody the virtues they seek to inspire in others, demonstrating balance, wisdom, and compassion in their actions. He stated, "The ruler who cultivates themselves brings harmony to their people," underscoring the connection between personal growth and effective leadership. This principle challenges contemporary leaders to prioritize self-cultivation and to lead with integrity and purpose.

Despite its emphasis on discipline and effort, Confucian integral formation is not without joy. Confucius observed, "The journey of self-cultivation is a source of delight, for in perfecting oneself, one contributes to the harmony of all." This teaching inspires individuals to approach their development with enthusiasm and gratitude, recognizing the profound satisfaction that comes from living in alignment with their values and purpose.

Ultimately, integral formation in Confucian philosophy is a path to becoming fully human, a process of harmonizing one's inner and outer worlds. It challenges individuals to cultivate their virtues, refine their intellect, and align their actions with the greater moral order. In the words of Confucius: "To perfect oneself is to perfect the world." By embracing this principle, we honor the Confucian legacy and create a foundation for enduring harmony, shared prosperity, and the flourishing of humanity.

Chapter 31
Moral Example

Within the fabric of Confucian thought, the concept of moral example shines as a guiding principle, radiating through generations as a cornerstone of ethical leadership and personal development. In Confucianism, a moral example is not merely an abstract ideal but a tangible expression of virtue, action, and influence. Through the alignment of one's thoughts, words, and deeds, a moral exemplar transforms ethical theory into lived practice, demonstrating the power of virtue to shape both individuals and society.

Confucius held that moral example begins with the individual but resonates outward like ripples in a still pond. "When the superior man acts with virtue," he taught, "his family follows, his state prospers, and harmony reigns in the world." This cascading effect underscores the interconnectedness of personal integrity and societal order. The moral example is not confined to the elite but is a universal aspiration, accessible to all who commit themselves to the cultivation of virtue.

The foundation of a moral example lies in **Ren** (humanity), the essence of benevolence and compassion. Confucius emphasized that the ability to empathize with others, to feel their joys and sorrows, is the hallmark of moral greatness. He advised, "Do not impose on others what you yourself do not desire," framing a golden standard for ethical behavior. Through Ren, the moral exemplar fosters relationships based on mutual respect and care, creating a social fabric rooted in trust and harmony.

Yet, humanity alone does not suffice. The moral example must also be grounded in **Yi** (justice), which ensures that actions are guided by a steadfast commitment to what is right. Yi transcends personal gain, anchoring decisions in principles of fairness and integrity. Confucius admired those who acted with righteousness even at great personal cost, declaring, "The superior man chooses the path of justice, though it be difficult, over the path of ease." Through Yi, the moral exemplar becomes a guardian of ethical standards, inspiring others to uphold justice in their own lives.

Li (ritual propriety) further enhances the moral example by providing a framework for consistent and respectful conduct. Rituals, in the Confucian sense, encompass not only formal ceremonies but also everyday acts of courtesy and decorum. By adhering to Li, the moral exemplar demonstrates the importance of discipline and attentiveness in social interactions, fostering a culture of mutual appreciation. Confucius observed, "Through rituals, we cultivate respect and harmony, which guide us in all things."

In addition to these virtues, the moral exemplar must possess **Zhi** (wisdom), the capacity to discern the best course of action in complex situations. Wisdom enables the moral leader to navigate ambiguity with clarity, ensuring that decisions are both ethical and practical. Confucius valued reflection as a path to wisdom, teaching, "By examining oneself daily, one gains insight into right and wrong." This emphasis on self-reflection highlights the role of introspection in refining the moral example.

The practice of moral example is vividly illustrated in the lives of Confucian disciples such as **Yan Hui**, Confucius's favorite student, who embodied humility, resilience, and an unwavering dedication to self-improvement. Despite living in poverty, Yan Hui's commitment to virtue never faltered, earning him the admiration of his peers and the lasting respect of Confucian tradition. His life serves as a testament to the enduring power of moral example to inspire and elevate.

Confucian teachings also emphasize the role of moral example in leadership. A ruler, Confucius believed, must govern not through coercion but through virtue, acting as a model for their subjects. "The ruler who leads with virtue," he stated, "is like the north star: steadfast and unwavering, drawing all others into alignment." This principle underscores the transformative potential of leadership grounded in ethical integrity, fostering loyalty and cooperation without the need for force.

The power of moral example extends beyond the individual or the leader. It is a force for collective transformation, encouraging entire communities to embrace virtuous living. In families, parents who model respect, diligence, and kindness lay the groundwork for their children's moral development. In societies, citizens who act with honesty and fairness inspire their peers to do the same, creating a culture of mutual accountability.

The Confucian concept of moral example remains deeply relevant in the modern world. In an era marked by ethical dilemmas and social challenges, the need for leaders and individuals who embody integrity has never been greater. Whether in politics, business, education, or personal life, the moral example provides a timeless framework for navigating complexity with virtue and wisdom.

For educators, the moral example is a cornerstone of teaching. Confucius himself believed that teachers must embody the values they wish to impart, stating, "The teacher inspires through example more than through words." This principle calls on educators to model diligence, curiosity, and respect, ensuring that their students learn not only knowledge but also the virtues essential for a fulfilling life.

For leaders, the moral example is a source of authority and legitimacy. A leader who governs with integrity earns the trust of their people, fostering stability and cooperation. Conversely, a leader who fails to embody ethical principles risks alienating their followers and eroding the social fabric. Confucius warned, "The ruler who lacks virtue cannot command loyalty, for trust is the foundation of governance."

In the context of family life, the moral example shapes the next generation, ensuring that the virtues of one era are passed on to the next. Parents who practice honesty, empathy, and responsibility teach their children to value these qualities, creating a legacy of ethical living. Confucius observed, "The family is the root of virtue; from it grows the harmony of the world."

The process of becoming a moral exemplar is not without its challenges. It requires discipline, self-awareness, and the courage to act with integrity even in the face of adversity. Yet, the rewards are profound, both for the individual and for those they influence. Confucius reassured his followers, "To walk the path of virtue may be demanding, but it is also the path of lasting fulfillment."

Ultimately, the moral example is not merely an ideal to be admired but a practice to be embraced. It challenges each individual to embody the virtues they wish to see in others, transforming ethical principles into lived reality. As Confucius taught, "The superior man seeks to perfect himself so that he may perfect the world." Through the power of moral example, we honor this timeless wisdom, creating a foundation for harmony, justice, and the flourishing of humanity.

Chapter 32
Applied Wisdom

In Confucian thought, wisdom is not a static accumulation of knowledge but a dynamic force that bridges understanding and action. Known as **Zhi**, wisdom is revered as the guiding principle that enables individuals to navigate the complexities of life with clarity, integrity, and purpose. It is a form of intelligence deeply rooted in ethical reflection, practical experience, and the alignment of actions with virtue. Confucius believed that wisdom, when applied, has the power to harmonize relationships, resolve conflicts, and elevate society as a whole.

Applied wisdom is not an abstract ideal. It manifests in everyday decisions, shaping the way individuals respond to challenges and opportunities. Confucius observed, "The wise person considers what is just and acts accordingly." This approach underscores the transformative nature of wisdom when it transcends theoretical contemplation and becomes a force for ethical action.

At the heart of applied wisdom is the Confucian ideal of balance. Wisdom enables individuals to navigate the tension between competing values or priorities, finding a harmonious path that serves the greater good. This balance is exemplified in the Confucian concept of **Zhongyong**, often translated as "the Doctrine of the Mean." Zhongyong emphasizes moderation and equilibrium, guiding individuals to avoid extremes and act in a manner that is both measured and appropriate. Confucius taught, "The wise man does not lean too far to either side; he walks the middle way, where harmony resides."

Wisdom in Confucianism is deeply relational. It is not pursued for personal gain or intellectual superiority but as a means of enhancing one's interactions with others. Wisdom enables individuals to understand the perspectives, needs, and motivations of those around them, fostering empathy and cooperation. This relational aspect of wisdom is captured in Confucius's advice: "To know others is wisdom; to know oneself is enlightenment." Through self-awareness and understanding, applied wisdom becomes a tool for building trust and strengthening communities.

In practice, applied wisdom manifests in three key areas: decision-making, conflict resolution, and leadership. In decision-making, wisdom provides a moral compass, ensuring that choices are aligned with ethical principles. Confucius emphasized the importance of reflection in this process, stating, "Study the past to understand the present and prepare for the future." By learning from historical and personal experiences, the wise individual develops the insight needed to navigate uncertainty and complexity.

Conflict resolution is another realm where applied wisdom is indispensable. Confucius viewed conflict not as a threat but as an opportunity for growth and reconciliation. He taught that wisdom enables individuals to approach disagreements with humility and a focus on common ground. "The superior man is conciliatory yet firm," he explained, highlighting the importance of balancing flexibility with adherence to principles. Through wise action, conflicts can be transformed into opportunities for deeper understanding and mutual respect.

In leadership, applied wisdom is a defining characteristic of the Confucian ideal ruler or administrator. A wise leader possesses the vision to see beyond immediate circumstances, the discernment to identify the best course of action, and the integrity to act for the benefit of all. Confucius stated, "A ruler who governs with wisdom is like a guiding star, steady and bright, inspiring those who follow." This emphasis on wisdom in leadership reflects the Confucian belief that governance is not merely about power but about moral responsibility and the cultivation of harmony.

Examples of applied wisdom abound in Confucian teachings and history. One such example is the story of King Wen of Zhou, who is celebrated for his ability to balance justice with compassion. Faced with a rebellious noble, King Wen sought to understand the underlying causes of discontent rather than resorting to harsh punishment. His decision to address the root of the issue, rather than its symptoms, not only resolved the conflict but also strengthened the loyalty of his subjects. This story illustrates how applied wisdom fosters lasting solutions and builds trust.

In daily life, applied wisdom is no less relevant. It guides individuals in managing personal relationships, making ethical choices, and contributing to the well-being of their communities. For example, a parent practicing applied wisdom considers not only the immediate needs of their child but also the long-term impact of their guidance. A teacher uses wisdom to adapt their methods to the unique strengths and challenges of each student. In each case, wisdom transforms routine actions into meaningful contributions to the growth and harmony of those involved.

Confucianism also emphasizes the cultivation of wisdom as an ongoing process. Wisdom is not innate but developed through study, reflection, and engagement with the world. Confucius himself exemplified this lifelong pursuit, stating, "At fifteen, I set my heart on learning; at thirty, I stood firm; at forty, I had no doubts; at fifty, I understood Heaven's will." This progression reflects the Confucian belief that wisdom deepens with time and experience, requiring patience and dedication.

The path to wisdom is illuminated by several practices central to Confucianism. First among these is **self-reflection**, a practice that Confucius regarded as essential for personal growth. He advised, "Examine yourself three times a day: Are my actions aligned with my duties? Are my words sincere? Have I fulfilled my commitments?" Through such introspection, individuals gain clarity about their strengths and areas for improvement, enabling them to act more wisely.

Another practice is the study of **texts and traditions**. Confucius believed that wisdom is enriched by engagement with the teachings of the past, which provide a foundation for understanding and application. The Confucian classics, such as the *Analects* and the *Book of Changes*, serve as timeless sources of guidance, offering insights into the nature of humanity, morality, and the cosmos. By studying these works, individuals develop a broader perspective that informs their decisions and actions.

The cultivation of wisdom requires **active participation in society**. Confucius viewed life itself as a classroom, where interactions with others provide opportunities for learning and growth. He taught, "One can learn from anyone: the virtuous inspire imitation, and the flawed offer lessons on what to avoid." This openness to learning from all experiences reflects the Confucian ideal of humility and adaptability, qualities that are integral to applied wisdom.

In the modern world, the relevance of applied wisdom is as profound as ever. In an era marked by rapid change and complex challenges, the ability to navigate uncertainty with clarity and ethical integrity is invaluable. Whether addressing issues such as climate change, social inequality, or personal dilemmas, applied wisdom provides a framework for thoughtful and responsible action.

Moreover, the emphasis on relational wisdom in Confucianism resonates in contemporary contexts. In a globalized society, understanding and empathy are crucial for building bridges across cultural and ideological divides. The Confucian principle of "seeking harmony without uniformity" offers a model for embracing diversity while fostering cooperation, highlighting the enduring significance of wisdom in creating a more inclusive world.

Ultimately, applied wisdom is the art of turning knowledge into action and virtue into impact. It challenges individuals to not only understand what is right but to act upon it, transforming ethical principles into tangible contributions to the well-being of others. As Confucius declared, "The wise are not content to know; they seek to do, for wisdom finds its fulfillment in action." Through this timeless insight, the Confucian vision of wisdom continues to inspire and guide, illuminating the path to a more harmonious and enlightened existence.

Chapter 33
Virtuous Politics

In the Confucian vision, politics is not a domain for the pursuit of power but a sacred responsibility rooted in virtue. The Confucian ideal of governance calls for leaders who embody ethical principles and who prioritize the welfare of the people above all else. It is a vision of politics as moral stewardship, where the ruler's actions set the tone for the harmony and prosperity of the entire society.

Virtuous politics begins with the principle of **benevolent rule**, or *Ren Zheng*, where leadership is grounded in humanity, compassion, and a deep sense of duty to others. Confucius believed that the legitimacy of any government depends not on coercion or fear but on the moral character of its leaders. He stated, "He who governs by virtue is like the north star: it remains in place, while all the stars revolve around it." In this metaphor, the virtuous ruler serves as a constant, guiding force, inspiring loyalty and order through moral authority rather than force.

Central to this philosophy is the Confucian concept of **Mandate of Heaven** (*Tianming*). This ancient idea asserts that a ruler's authority is granted by Heaven and is contingent upon their moral conduct. A virtuous ruler acts as a bridge between Heaven and Earth, ensuring that their governance aligns with cosmic principles of justice and harmony. However, this mandate is not permanent; it can be revoked if a leader fails to uphold ethical standards. Confucius explained, "Heaven sees as the people see; Heaven hears as the people hear." In this way, the well-being of the people becomes the ultimate measure of a leader's virtue and legitimacy.

The Confucian ideal ruler, often referred to as the **Sage-King**, is a person of exemplary moral character, wisdom, and self-discipline. Such a leader embodies the Confucian virtues of **Ren** (humanity), **Yi** (justice), **Li** (ritual propriety), and **Zhi** (wisdom), creating a government that reflects these values in its policies and practices. For Confucius, governance is an extension of personal morality; only by cultivating virtue within oneself can a ruler govern others effectively. He taught, "The superior man governs not by laws but by moral example, for when the ruler is virtuous, the people are naturally inclined toward goodness."

One of the core tenets of virtuous politics is the **promotion of harmony** (*He*). In Confucian thought, harmony is not the absence of conflict but the art of balancing diverse interests and perspectives to create a cohesive and flourishing society. A virtuous leader understands the importance of dialogue and consensus, striving to mediate disputes and foster unity without suppressing individuality. This emphasis on harmony extends to the relationship between government and people, where mutual respect and trust form the foundation of governance.

The Confucian model of virtuous politics also prioritizes **education** as a cornerstone of effective leadership. Confucius believed that an educated ruler is better equipped to make wise decisions and to inspire others through their knowledge and insight. Education, in this context, is not merely academic but moral, encompassing the study of ethics, history, and the Confucian classics. This comprehensive approach ensures that leaders develop both intellectual acuity and moral integrity. As Confucius stated, "To govern is to rectify; if you lead by example, the people will correct themselves."

Confucian politics is deeply committed to the principle of **meritocracy**. Leadership positions should be awarded based on virtue and competence, rather than hereditary privilege or wealth. This ideal was institutionalized during the Han dynasty through the civil service examination system, which sought to identify and promote talented individuals regardless of their social background. By valuing merit over status, Confucianism advocates for a government that reflects the highest ethical and intellectual standards.

In practice, virtuous politics involves creating policies that reflect the values of compassion, justice, and responsibility. A virtuous government prioritizes the welfare of its citizens, addressing their needs for security, education, and economic stability. Confucius emphasized the importance of meeting basic needs, stating, "Good governance provides sufficient food, military security, and the trust of the people." However, he argued that trust is the most essential of these elements, as it underpins the legitimacy and stability of any government.

Historical examples of virtuous politics in Confucian tradition highlight the transformative potential of ethical leadership. The reign of Emperor Taizong of the Tang dynasty is often cited as a model of Confucian governance. Known for his wisdom and compassion, Taizong sought the counsel of scholars, implemented fair taxation policies, and worked tirelessly to promote social harmony. His reign is remembered as a golden age of cultural and economic prosperity, illustrating the profound impact of virtuous leadership.

Confucianism also acknowledges the challenges of virtuous politics, particularly in times of corruption or moral decline. Confucius himself lived during the tumultuous Spring and Autumn period, a time marked by political instability and widespread unethical behavior among rulers. In response, he advocated for a return to moral principles, urging leaders to act as role models and to restore the ethical foundations of society. His teachings serve as a timeless reminder that virtuous politics requires both vigilance and commitment.

In the modern era, the relevance of Confucian virtuous politics extends beyond its historical context. Its emphasis on moral leadership, social harmony, and public trust offers valuable insights for addressing contemporary political challenges. Issues such as corruption, inequality, and environmental degradation demand a return to ethical governance that prioritizes the common good over personal or partisan interests. Confucian principles provide a framework for fostering accountability, transparency, and justice in political systems around the world.

Moreover, the Confucian focus on education and meritocracy resonates in today's globalized society, where the complexity of governance requires leaders with both expertise and ethical grounding. By investing in the cultivation of virtuous leaders, societies can build institutions that reflect the highest standards of integrity and competence.

Confucian virtuous politics is ultimately a vision of governance as service—a service to the people, to the principles of justice, and to the universal order. It challenges leaders to transcend self-interest and to act with courage, compassion, and wisdom. As Confucius declared, "The superior man thinks of virtue; the small man thinks of profit." This timeless teaching continues to inspire the pursuit of a politics that is not only effective but deeply humane, guiding humanity toward a more harmonious and enlightened future.

Chapter 34
Moral Leadership

At the heart of Confucian philosophy lies the principle of moral leadership, an ideal that transcends mere governance and delves into the ethical fabric of human relationships. Moral leadership is not defined by power, authority, or coercion, but by the ability of a leader to inspire, guide, and cultivate harmony through virtue. In Confucian thought, the essence of leadership lies in the cultivation of one's character and the embodiment of moral principles, ensuring that the ruler's influence radiates naturally and profoundly throughout society.

Confucius envisioned leadership as a moral obligation, where those in power must act as custodians of virtue, not merely enforcers of laws. He famously stated, "The superior man governs by moral force, not by law. He leads others with virtue, and they naturally follow." This philosophy underscores the belief that a society's harmony and stability depend on the ethical conduct of its leaders. When rulers act with integrity, they set an example that inspires trust, loyalty, and moral behavior among their subjects.

Central to Confucian moral leadership is the concept of the **Junzi**, or "superior person." The Junzi is an individual who embodies the highest virtues, including **Ren** (humanity), **Yi** (justice), **Li** (propriety), and **Xin** (trustworthiness). Such a person serves as a model of ethical conduct, demonstrating self-discipline, humility, and a commitment to the greater good. Confucius believed that the cultivation of Junzi qualities was essential for anyone aspiring to leadership, as these virtues form the foundation of moral authority.

The Confucian emphasis on **self-cultivation** as a prerequisite for leadership reflects the belief that a ruler cannot govern others without first mastering themselves. Confucius taught, "To govern others, one must first govern oneself." This principle highlights the interconnectedness of personal virtue and public service. A moral leader continuously strives for self-improvement, seeking to align their thoughts, words, and actions with ethical principles. This process of self-cultivation involves introspection, education, and the practice of virtue in daily life.

One of the defining characteristics of moral leadership is **Ren**, the virtue of humanity and compassion. Ren represents the capacity to empathize with others, to act with kindness, and to prioritize the well-being of the people. Confucius believed that a leader guided by Ren would naturally earn the respect and loyalty of their subjects, creating a government rooted in mutual trust and cooperation. He stated, "A ruler who practices humanity is like the sun shining on the people, warming them and guiding them toward growth."

Another cornerstone of moral leadership is **Yi**, or justice. Yi calls for a leader to act with righteousness, ensuring that their decisions are guided by fairness rather than self-interest. A moral leader must uphold justice even when it is difficult, demonstrating unwavering commitment to ethical principles. Confucius emphasized that justice is the foundation of trust in leadership, stating, "Without justice, a ruler cannot stand. The people will lose faith, and the harmony of the state will crumble."

The principle of **Li**, or propriety, further reinforces the moral framework of leadership. Li encompasses the rituals, traditions, and social norms that guide ethical behavior and promote harmony within society. A leader who adheres to Li demonstrates respect for the cultural and moral values of their community, fostering a sense of order and unity. Confucius observed that when leaders practice Li with sincerity, they cultivate a culture of respect and reverence, which strengthens social bonds.

Confucian moral leadership also demands **accountability** and **humility**. A leader must recognize their responsibility to serve the people and to act as a steward of their well-being. This sense of duty is reflected in Confucius's teaching, "The ruler is like the wind, and the people are like grass. When the wind blows, the grass bends." This metaphor illustrates the profound influence of a leader's character and actions on the behavior of their subjects. It also serves as a reminder that leaders bear the ultimate responsibility for the moral and social fabric of their society.

In historical contexts, the concept of moral leadership found its expression in the Confucian ideal of the **Sage-King**, a ruler who governs with wisdom, virtue, and benevolence. Examples of such leadership are celebrated in Chinese history, including the reigns of Emperor Yao and Emperor Shun, who were revered for their ethical governance and dedication to the welfare of their people. These leaders exemplified the Confucian belief that moral authority is the most enduring and effective form of power.

The Confucian emphasis on education further underscores the role of moral leadership. Education is seen as the foundation for cultivating virtue and wisdom, equipping leaders with the knowledge and ethical grounding necessary to navigate complex challenges. Confucius declared, "By studying the past, one can understand the present. By cultivating wisdom, one can govern with foresight." This approach to education integrates moral philosophy with practical governance, ensuring that leaders are both principled and capable.

Confucian moral leadership is not limited to rulers; it extends to all levels of society. In Confucian thought, parents, teachers, and community leaders are all entrusted with the responsibility of leading by example and fostering virtue in those they influence. This decentralized vision of moral leadership creates a ripple effect, where the cultivation of ethical behavior at every level contributes to the harmony and prosperity of the entire society.

In modern times, the principles of Confucian moral leadership remain relevant as a guide for ethical governance and responsible leadership. In an era marked by political polarization, corruption, and social inequality, the Confucian emphasis on virtue, justice, and compassion offers a timeless framework for addressing these challenges. Leaders who prioritize the common good, act with integrity, and inspire trust can foster greater social cohesion and resilience.

Moreover, the Confucian ideal of leadership transcends cultural boundaries, offering universal lessons on the importance of ethical conduct in positions of power. Whether applied in politics, business, or community leadership, the principles of moral leadership serve as a reminder that true authority stems not from dominance but from the ability to inspire and uplift others.

Confucian moral leadership is a profound expression of the belief that leaders have a sacred duty to serve as stewards of virtue and harmony. It challenges leaders to rise above personal ambition and to act with wisdom, justice, and compassion. As Confucius observed, "The virtue of the superior man is like the wind; the virtue of the small man is like the grass. When the wind passes over it, the grass must bend." This enduring metaphor encapsulates the essence of moral leadership, where the power of virtue shapes the destiny of societies and guides humanity toward a more harmonious and ethical future.

Chapter 35
Social Order

Confucian philosophy places the concept of social order at the heart of a harmonious society. For Confucius, the ideal society was one in which each individual understood and fulfilled their role within a clearly defined hierarchy, guided by mutual respect and adherence to moral principles. Social order, as envisioned in Confucian thought, is not imposed by force or coercion but is cultivated through the practice of virtue, the observance of rituals, and the nurturing of harmonious relationships.

At the core of Confucian social order is the idea of **hierarchy**. Confucius viewed society as a network of interconnected relationships, each governed by specific roles and responsibilities. These roles were not arbitrary but were rooted in natural and moral principles. For instance, the relationship between a ruler and their subjects mirrored the relationship between a parent and their child, emphasizing care, guidance, and mutual respect. Confucius believed that when each individual fulfilled their role with virtue, the entire society would function harmoniously.

The concept of the **Five Relationships (Wu Lun)** serves as the foundation of Confucian social order. These relationships—ruler and subject, father and son, husband and wife, elder brother and younger brother, and friend and friend—are hierarchical yet reciprocal. Each party in these relationships has specific duties, and their fulfillment creates a balance that sustains the social fabric. For example, a ruler is expected to govern with justice and benevolence, while subjects are expected to respond with loyalty and obedience. Similarly, parents are expected to provide love and guidance, while children are expected to show filial piety and respect.

The Confucian virtue of **Li**, or propriety, plays a critical role in maintaining social order. Li encompasses the rituals, customs, and social norms that govern behavior, ensuring that individuals act in ways that uphold harmony and respect. These rituals extend beyond formal ceremonies to include everyday interactions, such as greeting others with courtesy, observing familial duties, and showing deference to elders. By practicing Li, individuals internalize their roles within the social hierarchy and contribute to a sense of unity and order.

Another essential aspect of social order in Confucian thought is the cultivation of **virtue (De)**. Confucius emphasized that the stability of a society depends on the moral character of its members, particularly those in positions of authority. A virtuous ruler inspires virtue in their subjects, creating a ripple effect that strengthens the moral foundation of the entire community. This idea is encapsulated in the saying, "When the ruler is righteous, all beneath heaven will be righteous."

The concept of **harmony (He)** further reinforces the Confucian vision of social order. Harmony does not imply uniformity or the absence of conflict but rather the balance and integration of diverse elements within a society. Confucius taught that harmony arises when individuals respect differences, prioritize the common good, and act with consideration for others. This principle applies not only to interpersonal relationships but also to the governance of states, where policies should aim to reconcile competing interests and promote collective well-being.

Education is another pillar of Confucian social order. Confucius believed that the cultivation of knowledge and virtue was essential for individuals to fulfill their social roles effectively. Through education, people learn to discern right from wrong, develop moral character, and understand their responsibilities within the social hierarchy. Confucius famously stated, "Education breeds confidence; confidence breeds hope; hope breeds peace." This progression underscores the transformative power of education in fostering a harmonious and orderly society.

Confucian social order also emphasizes the importance of **reciprocity (Shu)**. This principle, often expressed as the Golden Rule—"Do not do to others what you would not want done to yourself"—encourages individuals to act with empathy and consideration. Reciprocity fosters trust and mutual respect, strengthening the bonds that hold society together. It also serves as a moral compass, guiding individuals to act in ways that contribute to the greater good.

Historically, the Confucian model of social order deeply influenced Chinese governance and culture. During the Han dynasty, Confucian principles became the official ideology of the state, shaping laws, education, and administrative practices. The hierarchical structure of Confucianism provided a framework for organizing society, from the family unit to the imperial court. Rituals and ceremonies reinforced social roles and instilled a sense of continuity and tradition.

However, Confucian social order has also faced criticism and challenges, particularly in modern times. Critics argue that its emphasis on hierarchy and conformity can perpetuate inequality and stifle individual expression. For instance, the rigid gender roles prescribed in traditional Confucianism have been questioned in the context of contemporary movements for gender equality. Similarly, the principle of filial piety, while fostering strong family bonds, can place excessive burdens on individuals, particularly in societies with aging populations.

Despite these challenges, the principles of Confucian social order remain relevant in addressing contemporary issues. In an age of globalization and cultural diversity, the Confucian emphasis on harmony, mutual respect, and moral leadership offers valuable insights for building inclusive and cohesive societies. The concept of balance, central to Confucian thought, can guide efforts to reconcile individual rights with collective responsibilities, tradition with innovation, and cultural diversity with social unity.

Confucian social order also provides a framework for addressing the ethical dimensions of leadership and governance. In a world grappling with issues such as corruption, inequality, and environmental degradation, the Confucian ideals of virtue, justice, and compassion serve as a reminder that true leadership is grounded in moral integrity and a commitment to the common good.

In practical terms, the principles of Confucian social order can be applied to various contexts, from family relationships to organizational management. For example, businesses and institutions can benefit from the Confucian emphasis on ethical leadership, clear roles and responsibilities, and the cultivation of trust and reciprocity among members. Educational systems can draw on Confucian values to promote character development and social responsibility alongside academic achievement.

Ultimately, Confucian social order is a vision of a harmonious society in which individuals and communities thrive through mutual respect, moral integrity, and a shared commitment to the common good. It challenges us to see ourselves not as isolated individuals but as interconnected members of a larger whole, each with a role to play in sustaining the balance and vitality of the social fabric. As Confucius observed, "When there is order in the family, there is harmony in the state; when there is harmony in the state, there is peace in the world." This timeless wisdom invites us to reflect on the principles that underpin our own communities and to strive for a world in which harmony and justice prevail.

Chapter 36
Public Administration

Confucianism provides a framework for public administration that blends ethical governance with practical efficiency. At its core lies the conviction that a well-governed state is built on the moral character of its leaders and the cultivation of virtues among its people. Public administration, in the Confucian sense, is not merely about bureaucratic management but about embodying principles that align with harmony, justice, and the greater good.

Central to Confucian public administration is the concept of **moral leadership**. Confucius emphasized that a ruler or administrator should lead by example, displaying qualities such as benevolence, integrity, and self-discipline. He declared, "The virtue of the superior man is like the wind; the virtue of the small man is like the grass. When the wind passes over it, the grass must bend." This metaphor illustrates how the moral conduct of those in power sets the tone for the rest of society, inspiring ethical behavior at all levels.

The **Mandate of Heaven (Tianming)**, an enduring concept in Confucian thought, underscores the moral foundation of public administration. It holds that rulers derive their legitimacy from their ability to govern justly and uphold the welfare of their people. This mandate is not a divine right but a conditional privilege, contingent on the ruler's virtue and effectiveness. A failure to maintain moral governance results in the loss of this mandate, which Confucians interpreted as natural disasters, rebellions, or societal decline—signals of divine displeasure and the need for reform.

A key element of Confucian administration is the cultivation of **meritocracy**. Confucius believed that positions of power should be granted based on ability and virtue rather than inherited privilege or wealth. This belief was institutionalized in the form of the Imperial Examination System during later dynasties, where candidates were tested on their knowledge of Confucian texts, ethical reasoning, and practical governance. By emphasizing merit, Confucianism sought to ensure that public officials possessed not only intellectual acumen but also a commitment to the common good.

The role of **education** in public administration cannot be overstated in Confucian thought. Education serves as the foundation for cultivating virtuous leaders who possess both the wisdom to govern and the ethical compass to prioritize the welfare of their people. Confucius asserted that education should develop both moral character and practical skills, creating administrators who are as compassionate as they are competent. Through education, leaders learn to balance the competing demands of governance, such as economic development, social stability, and environmental stewardship.

Confucianism also emphasizes the importance of **rituals (Li)** in public administration. Rituals serve as more than ceremonial practices; they create a sense of order, continuity, and respect for authority within governance structures. Rituals also ensure that administrators maintain a sense of humility and responsibility, reminding them of their duty to serve the people rather than pursue personal gain. For instance, ceremonies honoring ancestors or expressing gratitude for a bountiful harvest connect the state to its cultural and moral heritage, reinforcing the legitimacy of its leadership.

Another fundamental aspect of Confucian public administration is the pursuit of **justice (Yi)**. In a Confucian state, justice transcends legalism and procedural fairness; it reflects a deeper commitment to ethical principles and the well-being of all citizens. Confucius taught that laws alone cannot ensure justice. Instead, leaders must cultivate moral discernment, making decisions that align with the spirit of fairness and humanity. "The noble-minded are calm and steady," Confucius observed, "while small-minded individuals are forever consumed by anxiety." A just leader, guided by inner virtue, acts with clarity and decisiveness to address the needs of the people.

The Confucian principle of **reciprocity (Shu)** also informs public administration. Administrators are expected to treat citizens with the same respect and care that they would wish to receive. This principle fosters trust between the government and the governed, creating a collaborative relationship in which both parties work toward the collective good. The trust engendered by reciprocity is vital for maintaining social stability and encouraging civic participation.

In practice, Confucian public administration prioritizes **harmonious governance**, which balances authority with compassion and pragmatism. This harmony extends to all levels of administration, from national policies to local governance. Confucius envisioned a state in which administrators actively engage with their communities, listening to their concerns and addressing their needs with sensitivity and efficiency. The ideal administrator acts as a bridge between the people and the state, ensuring that governance reflects the collective values and aspirations of society.

Confucianism also recognizes the importance of **environmental stewardship** in public administration. Ancient Confucian texts frequently reference the interconnectedness of humanity and nature, urging leaders to protect the natural world as an integral part of their duty. This perspective aligns with modern principles of sustainable development, emphasizing the need for policies that balance economic growth with ecological preservation.

Historically, Confucian principles shaped the administrative practices of various Chinese dynasties, particularly during the Han and Tang periods. Bureaucratic institutions were structured around Confucian ideals, emphasizing hierarchical organization, meritocratic recruitment, and ethical governance.

While these systems were not without flaws, they provided a model for stability and continuity that influenced neighboring cultures in Korea, Japan, and Vietnam.

However, the Confucian approach to public administration has faced challenges and criticisms in modern times. Critics argue that its emphasis on hierarchy and tradition can stifle innovation and adaptability in rapidly changing societies. Additionally, the reliance on virtue as a criterion for leadership has been criticized for its potential subjectivity, raising concerns about accountability and transparency.

Despite these critiques, Confucian principles remain relevant in addressing contemporary governance issues. The emphasis on ethical leadership, civic responsibility, and environmental sustainability resonates with global efforts to create more equitable and resilient societies. For instance, Confucian ideals can inform debates on corruption by highlighting the importance of moral integrity in public office. Similarly, the principle of reciprocity can guide initiatives to rebuild trust between governments and citizens in polarized or fragmented societies.

In practical terms, Confucian public administration offers a blueprint for creating governance systems that prioritize human dignity, social harmony, and the collective good. By integrating ethical considerations into policy-making, leaders can ensure that their decisions reflect the values and aspirations of their communities. The Confucian vision challenges administrators to move beyond technocratic efficiency and embrace a holistic approach that addresses the moral, cultural, and spiritual dimensions of governance.

Ultimately, Confucian public administration reminds us that governance is not merely a mechanism for managing resources or enforcing laws. It is a moral endeavor, rooted in the shared responsibility to nurture a just and harmonious society. As Confucius himself observed, "To rule a country of a thousand chariots, one must be attentive to business, sincere in speech, moderate in spending, and love the people." These timeless words invite modern administrators to reflect on their roles as stewards of both the present and the future, striving to create a world where virtue and justice prevail.

Chapter 37
The Common Good

At the heart of Confucian philosophy lies an unwavering commitment to the concept of the common good, a vision of society where the welfare of the collective takes precedence over individual desires. The common good, in Confucian terms, is not simply a pragmatic goal but a moral imperative, deeply rooted in the interconnectedness of human lives and the shared pursuit of harmony. It serves as the cornerstone of governance, family relations, and societal development, reflecting an intricate balance between personal cultivation and collective responsibility.

The Confucian conception of the common good begins with the cultivation of **Ren** (humaneness). Ren is the guiding virtue that inspires individuals to act with compassion and empathy, forming the ethical foundation for relationships that prioritize the well-being of others. Confucius taught, "Do not impose on others what you yourself do not desire." This principle, a precursor to the Golden Rule, underscores the moral obligation to consider how one's actions affect others, aligning personal conduct with the greater needs of society.

Central to the Confucian vision of the common good is the **role of leadership**. Leaders are tasked with embodying virtues that inspire trust and cooperation among the people they serve. Confucius emphasized that a ruler's primary responsibility is to act as a moral exemplar, guiding the populace not through force or coercion but through virtuous action. "If a ruler is upright," Confucius observed, "all will go well without orders. If he is not upright, even when he gives orders, they will not be obeyed." This insight highlights the transformative power of ethical leadership in fostering a society oriented toward collective well-being.

The pursuit of the common good also demands a commitment to **justice (Yi)**. For Confucius, justice transcends mere legal frameworks; it embodies a moral discernment that ensures fairness and equity in the distribution of resources, opportunities, and responsibilities. Justice is not about rigid adherence to rules but about understanding the needs and circumstances of others, ensuring that societal structures serve everyone equitably. This principle requires leaders to act with integrity and impartiality, addressing social disparities and prioritizing the needs of the vulnerable.

Harmony (He) is another pillar of the common good in Confucian thought. Harmony does not imply uniformity but the coexistence of diverse elements in a balanced and mutually supportive relationship. In society, harmony is achieved when individuals fulfill their roles and responsibilities while respecting the roles of others. This dynamic balance promotes cooperation and reduces conflict, creating an environment where the collective can thrive. Confucius asserted that harmony in relationships, whether within the family, community, or government, forms the basis for a flourishing society.

The family, often described as the microcosm of society, is central to the Confucian understanding of the common good. **Filial piety (Xiao)**, the respect and care for one's parents and ancestors, is regarded as the foundation of social harmony. Confucius taught that by cultivating strong family bonds, individuals learn the values of respect, responsibility, and altruism, which they then extend to broader societal relationships. A harmonious family serves as the training ground for virtuous citizens who contribute to the common good with empathy and dedication.

Education plays a pivotal role in shaping a society committed to the common good. For Confucius, education is not solely about acquiring knowledge but about cultivating virtue and wisdom. It is through education that individuals learn to balance their personal aspirations with the needs of others, developing the moral clarity required to make decisions that benefit the collective. By promoting lifelong learning and self-reflection, Confucianism empowers individuals to contribute meaningfully to societal well-being.

The Confucian emphasis on **rituals (Li)** further reinforces the common good by creating structures that promote social cohesion and shared values. Rituals, in the Confucian sense, are not merely ceremonial but deeply symbolic acts that foster a sense of belonging and continuity within the community. They remind individuals of their interconnectedness and their obligations to others, encouraging behavior that aligns with the collective interest. From rites of passage to state ceremonies, these practices strengthen the bonds that hold society together.

The principle of **reciprocity (Shu)** is another critical component of the common good in Confucianism. Reciprocity calls for mutual respect and consideration, creating relationships built on trust and cooperation. It ensures that individuals act not out of self-interest but with an awareness of how their actions affect others. Confucius emphasized that reciprocity is essential for maintaining social harmony, as it encourages individuals to see themselves as part of a larger whole, where each person's well-being is tied to the well-being of others.

Confucianism's focus on the common good also extends to the realm of governance. A Confucian state is one where policies are crafted to benefit the majority while safeguarding the rights of minorities. This requires leaders to engage in **benevolent governance (Ren Zheng)**, prioritizing the needs of the people over personal or political gain. Benevolent governance is guided by the belief that the legitimacy of authority is derived from the leader's ability to promote the common good, reflecting the values of fairness, compassion, and inclusivity.

The Confucian approach to the common good also addresses the relationship between humanity and the natural world. Ancient Confucian texts frequently highlight the importance of living in harmony with nature, recognizing that environmental stewardship is integral to the well-being of society. This perspective aligns with contemporary principles of sustainable development, emphasizing that the pursuit of progress must not come at the expense of future generations.

Throughout history, Confucian ideals of the common good have inspired social reforms and policies aimed at reducing inequality and promoting justice. For example, the Confucian emphasis on meritocracy laid the foundation for systems of governance that prioritize talent and virtue over inherited privilege. Similarly, Confucian teachings have influenced community-based approaches to problem-solving, fostering a spirit of collective responsibility and mutual aid.

However, the pursuit of the common good in Confucianism is not without its challenges. Critics have pointed to the potential for hierarchical structures to concentrate power in ways that may undermine equality. Others argue that the emphasis on conformity to social roles can suppress individual autonomy and creativity. These critiques highlight the need for a nuanced understanding of how Confucian principles can be adapted to address the complexities of modern societies.

Despite these challenges, the Confucian vision of the common good offers valuable insights for addressing contemporary issues. In an age marked by growing inequality, political polarization, and environmental crises, Confucianism reminds us of the importance of prioritizing collective well-being over narrow self-interests. Its principles of ethical leadership, reciprocity, and harmony provide a framework for fostering trust, cooperation, and inclusivity in diverse and interconnected societies.

The Confucian ideal of the common good challenges us to look beyond individual aspirations and consider how our actions contribute to the broader tapestry of human life. It calls for a profound commitment to virtue, wisdom, and compassion, urging individuals and leaders alike to act with integrity and purpose. As Confucius wisely observed, "The strength of a nation is derived not from the wealth of its ruler but from the goodness of its people." This enduring truth serves as a beacon for those striving to create a world where the common good is not an abstract ideal but a lived reality.

Chapter 38
Governmental Justice

In Confucian philosophy, justice (**Yi**) forms the moral backbone of governance and is an essential pillar of societal harmony. It is not confined to the rigid enforcement of laws or the mechanical application of policies. Instead, governmental justice embodies the principle of doing what is right, ensuring fairness, and upholding the dignity of all members of society. Justice, in the Confucian context, is inseparably tied to ethical leadership and the moral cultivation of those who govern.

Confucius taught that a just government arises from the virtues of its rulers. A leader's moral integrity directly influences the righteousness of their administration. This relationship is captured in the Analects, where Confucius stated, "If a ruler is just, the people will naturally follow his example." Justice is therefore not imposed by force but flows organically from the moral example set by those in power. For Confucius, justice begins with the self-cultivation of leaders, whose virtuous behavior inspires trust and loyalty among their subjects.

The Confucian ideal of justice emphasizes **meritocracy**, where individuals are chosen for their roles in society based on talent, virtue, and competence rather than lineage or wealth. This principle was revolutionary for its time, challenging the hereditary systems that dominated ancient China. By advocating for the selection of officials based on their ability to govern wisely and justly, Confucianism laid the groundwork for an administrative system that sought fairness and efficiency. This approach aimed to create a government where policies were enacted with the welfare of the people in mind, ensuring that justice served the collective good rather than the interests of the elite.

Impartiality is another cornerstone of Confucian governmental justice. Justice requires leaders to act without bias, treating all individuals with fairness regardless of their social status or personal connections. Confucius warned against favoritism and corruption, recognizing that such practices erode public trust and destabilize society. In the Analects, he criticized rulers who prioritized personal gain over their responsibilities to the people, emphasizing that true justice demands selflessness and unwavering commitment to ethical principles.

In addition to impartiality, Confucian justice stresses the importance of **rectification of names (Zheng Ming)**. This principle advocates for clarity and consistency in the roles and responsibilities of individuals within society. For Confucius, societal harmony depends on people fulfilling their designated roles with integrity. A ruler must govern justly, a minister must serve loyally, and citizens must respect the laws and customs of the land. When roles are performed correctly, justice prevails, creating a stable and harmonious society. However, when these roles are neglected or misused, injustice and disorder follow.

The administration of justice in Confucian governance extends beyond punishment for wrongdoing. It involves **moral education** and the cultivation of virtue among citizens. Confucius believed that laws alone are insufficient to ensure justice; they must be complemented by moral guidance. As he stated, "If people are led by laws and coerced by punishment, they will try to avoid the punishment but have no sense of shame. If they are led by virtue and regulated by propriety, they will develop a sense of shame and become upright." This approach underscores the importance of nurturing a collective conscience, where individuals internalize ethical values and act justly out of moral conviction rather than fear of reprisal.

Confucian justice also places great emphasis on the protection of the vulnerable. In a just government, leaders must prioritize the welfare of those who are most at risk, including the poor, the elderly, and the marginalized. This commitment reflects the Confucian belief in **Ren** (humaneness) as the guiding principle of governance. Justice is not achieved by treating everyone identically but by addressing inequalities and ensuring that all members of society have the opportunity to thrive. A ruler's compassion and attentiveness to the needs of the vulnerable are seen as the ultimate measures of their moral character.

The balance between punishment and forgiveness is another critical aspect of Confucian justice. While Confucius acknowledged the necessity of laws and penalties to maintain order, he cautioned against their overuse. Excessive punishment, he argued, breeds resentment and undermines trust in the government. Instead, leaders should strive for a balanced approach that emphasizes rehabilitation and reconciliation. By addressing the root causes of misconduct and guiding individuals toward moral improvement, justice becomes a means of fostering harmony rather than perpetuating conflict.

Confucian justice is deeply intertwined with the concept of **He** (harmony). Unlike Western notions of justice, which often focus on retribution or the assertion of individual rights, Confucian justice seeks to restore balance and promote social cohesion. This approach reflects the broader Confucian worldview, where harmony is valued above conflict, and the interests of the collective are prioritized over individual grievances. Justice, in this context, is not merely the resolution of disputes but the creation of conditions that prevent discord from arising in the first place.

Historically, Confucian principles of justice influenced the development of legal and administrative systems in China and beyond. The Confucian-inspired meritocratic examination system, for instance, sought to ensure that government officials were selected based on their knowledge and virtue. This system, though not without its flaws, represented an early attempt to align governance with the ideals of fairness and competence. Similarly, Confucian teachings shaped the ethical frameworks of leaders, encouraging them to approach their duties with a sense of responsibility and compassion.

The legacy of Confucian justice continues to resonate in modern governance. Its emphasis on ethical leadership, fairness, and the welfare of the vulnerable offers valuable insights for addressing contemporary challenges. In an era marked by corruption, inequality, and social unrest, the Confucian vision of justice reminds us of the importance of prioritizing the common good and fostering trust between leaders and citizens.

However, the application of Confucian justice in modern contexts requires careful consideration. Critics have noted that its emphasis on hierarchy and social roles can perpetuate existing inequalities if not adapted to contemporary values of equality and human rights. Additionally, the reliance on moral education and virtuous leadership, while noble in theory, may be difficult to achieve in practice. These challenges underscore the need to reinterpret Confucian principles in ways that address the complexities of today's societies.

Despite these challenges, the core tenets of Confucian justice—ethical leadership, fairness, and compassion—remain profoundly relevant. They serve as a reminder that justice is not an abstract concept but a lived practice that requires continuous effort and reflection. By aligning governance with the principles of virtue and humanity, Confucianism offers a timeless blueprint for creating societies where justice is not merely enforced but deeply felt and universally upheld.

As Confucius observed, "The administration of justice lies in ensuring that all things are in their proper place." This simple yet profound statement encapsulates the essence of Confucian justice—a vision of governance where ethical principles guide every action, and the welfare of all is safeguarded through fairness, integrity, and compassion. In striving for such justice, we honor the enduring wisdom of Confucius and his vision of a harmonious and equitable world.

Chapter 39
Political Harmony

Confucian philosophy positions harmony (**He**) as the cornerstone of a well-functioning society, extending its influence beyond personal relationships to encompass the political realm. Political harmony is not merely the absence of conflict or the maintenance of superficial order; it is the active cultivation of balance, cooperation, and mutual respect among diverse groups and interests within the state. This ideal lies at the heart of Confucian governance, shaping its vision of ethical leadership, responsible administration, and the collective pursuit of the common good.

The Confucian vision of political harmony begins with the cultivation of virtue among leaders. For Confucius, the personal morality of those in power directly influences the stability and harmony of the political system. Leaders who embody virtues such as **Ren** (benevolence), **Yi** (righteousness), and **Li** (propriety) inspire trust and loyalty among the populace, creating a foundation for harmonious governance. The Analects capture this principle succinctly: "When the ruler is virtuous, the people will naturally follow." This belief underscores the transformative power of ethical leadership, where the ruler's conduct serves as a moral compass for the entire society.

At the core of Confucian political harmony lies the principle of **Zhong Yong**, often translated as the "Doctrine of the Mean." This principle advocates for balance and moderation in all aspects of governance, avoiding extremes that could destabilize the political order. In practice, Zhong Yong encourages leaders to navigate conflicts and competing interests with wisdom and impartiality, ensuring that decisions promote the long-term well-being of the state rather than short-term gains or partisan agendas. By adhering to this principle, leaders create a political environment where differing perspectives can coexist harmoniously, fostering unity amidst diversity.

One of the most significant aspects of Confucian political harmony is its emphasis on **dialogue and consensus-building**. Rather than imposing policies unilaterally, Confucian governance encourages open communication and collaborative decision-making. This approach reflects the belief that harmony is achieved through mutual understanding and the reconciliation of differences. Leaders are expected to listen to the concerns of their constituents, consider diverse viewpoints, and seek common ground that benefits all members of society. In the Confucian framework, the role of the government is not to dominate but to mediate, guiding the state toward collective harmony through inclusive and empathetic leadership.

The concept of political harmony also extends to the relationship between the ruler and the governed. In Confucianism, this relationship is framed as a reciprocal bond of mutual responsibility. The ruler is expected to govern with compassion and fairness, prioritizing the welfare of the people above personal interests. In return, the people are expected to show loyalty and respect toward the ruler. This dynamic creates a moral contract that binds the government and its citizens together in a shared commitment to the common good. When rulers fail to uphold their ethical responsibilities, however, Confucianism recognizes the legitimacy of dissent, viewing it as a necessary check on injustice and a means of restoring harmony.

Historical examples illustrate how Confucian principles of political harmony were applied in practice. During the Han dynasty, Confucianism was adopted as the guiding ideology of the state, shaping policies and administrative practices. The civil service examination system, rooted in Confucian values, sought to ensure that government officials were selected based on merit and virtue rather than wealth or lineage. This system fostered a sense of fairness and accountability, contributing to the stability and cohesion of the empire. Similarly, Confucian-inspired rituals and ceremonies reinforced social unity by emphasizing shared values and collective identity.

However, the pursuit of political harmony is not without challenges. One of the most significant obstacles is the tension between hierarchy and equality. Confucianism upholds a hierarchical vision of society, where each individual fulfills a specific role within a structured social order. While this hierarchy is intended to promote harmony by clarifying responsibilities and relationships, it can also perpetuate inequality and exclusion if not tempered by principles of fairness and compassion. Modern interpretations of Confucian political harmony must address this tension, ensuring that the pursuit of order does not come at the expense of justice or inclusivity.

Another challenge lies in balancing unity with diversity. Political harmony requires the integration of multiple perspectives and interests, but this process can be fraught with conflict and compromise. Confucianism offers valuable insights for navigating these complexities, emphasizing the importance of **Ren** (empathy) and **Li** (ritual propriety) as tools for fostering mutual respect and understanding. By approaching differences with humility and a genuine commitment to the common good, leaders can transform potential sources of division into opportunities for collaboration and growth.

In the modern context, Confucian principles of political harmony hold significant relevance for addressing global challenges. In an era marked by polarization, inequality, and environmental crises, the Confucian emphasis on ethical leadership, dialogue, and collective responsibility offers a compelling framework for building more inclusive and sustainable political systems. For instance, Confucian teachings on the balance between individual rights and collective welfare can inform contemporary debates on social justice, environmental stewardship, and global governance.

Moreover, the Confucian focus on moral education highlights the importance of cultivating virtues such as empathy, integrity, and civic responsibility among both leaders and citizens. By fostering a culture of ethical awareness, societies can create the conditions for political harmony to flourish. This approach underscores the interconnectedness of personal morality and public governance, reminding us that the pursuit of harmony begins within the hearts and minds of individuals.

Despite its enduring relevance, the application of Confucian political harmony in the modern world requires careful adaptation. Critics have noted that traditional Confucian governance often prioritized stability over innovation, potentially stifling creativity and dissent. To address this limitation, contemporary interpretations of Confucianism must embrace a more dynamic vision of harmony—one that values flexibility, adaptability, and the transformative potential of constructive conflict. By doing so, Confucianism can remain a vital source of wisdom for navigating the complexities of modern politics.

Ultimately, political harmony in the Confucian tradition is not an endpoint but a continuous process. It requires ongoing effort, reflection, and collaboration to balance competing interests, resolve conflicts, and uphold ethical principles. This dynamic vision of harmony reflects the broader Confucian worldview, where the pursuit of balance and order is both a personal and collective endeavor. As Confucius himself observed, "Harmony is the way of Heaven, and those who follow it bring peace to the world."

In striving for political harmony, we are reminded of our shared humanity and our responsibility to one another. By cultivating virtue, fostering dialogue, and prioritizing the common good, Confucianism offers a timeless blueprint for building societies where justice, compassion, and unity prevail. As we confront the challenges of the 21st century, the principles of Confucian political harmony remain a beacon of hope, guiding us toward a more equitable and harmonious world.

Chapter 40
Social Reform

Social reform, as envisioned within the Confucian tradition, is not a radical upheaval but a deliberate and ethical transformation aimed at restoring harmony to society. This approach stems from a foundational belief that disorder arises from moral decay and a failure to uphold virtues. Therefore, Confucian social reform seeks to realign societal structures with the principles of **Ren** (benevolence), **Yi** (righteousness), and **Li** (ritual propriety), creating a just and harmonious order for all individuals.

The Confucian path to social reform begins with the cultivation of individual virtue. For Confucius, moral transformation at the personal level is the foundation upon which broader societal change is built. He taught that leaders, in particular, must serve as paragons of virtue, demonstrating ethical behavior and inspiring those they govern to follow suit. This principle is captured in his famous dictum, "To put the world in order, we must first put the nation in order; to put the nation in order, we must first put the family in order; to put the family in order, we must first cultivate our personal lives."

Reforming society, then, is not solely the responsibility of governments or institutions but a collective endeavor that begins with individuals and families. The Confucian ideal of **Xiao** (filial piety) emphasizes the family as the cornerstone of moral development and social cohesion. A family that practices respect, care, and responsibility serves as a microcosm of a harmonious society, setting a moral example that radiates outward to the community and the state. By strengthening familial bonds and instilling virtues within the home, Confucianism asserts, society can be gradually reformed from its roots.

However, Confucian social reform is not confined to moral education alone; it also entails addressing systemic injustices that disrupt harmony. The Confucian concept of **Zhengming**, or "the rectification of names," offers a framework for reforming social roles and institutions. According to this principle, societal harmony depends on individuals fulfilling their roles and responsibilities according to their true essence. A ruler must act as a ruler, a parent as a parent, and so forth. When roles are misunderstood or misused—when a ruler governs selfishly, for instance—disorder ensues. Rectifying these misalignments involves both personal accountability and structural reforms to ensure that roles are clearly defined and ethically executed.

A pivotal aspect of Confucian social reform is its emphasis on education as a transformative force. Confucius himself was a tireless advocate for education, believing it to be the primary means of cultivating virtue and enabling individuals to fulfill their roles effectively. In a reformed society, education must extend beyond technical or vocational training to include moral instruction and the study of the classics, which provide timeless lessons on ethics and governance. By educating both leaders and citizens in the principles of Confucian thought, society can cultivate a culture of wisdom, integrity, and collective responsibility.

Historical examples highlight how Confucian principles of social reform have been applied in practice. During the Tang dynasty, Confucian ideals were used to shape legal codes and administrative practices, creating a governance system that emphasized justice and fairness. Similarly, the establishment of the imperial examination system during the Han dynasty allowed individuals from diverse backgrounds to ascend to positions of power based on merit rather than privilege. These reforms reflected the Confucian commitment to equity and accountability, ensuring that governance served the interests of all rather than the elite few.

Yet Confucian social reform is not without its challenges. One of its most significant obstacles is the tension between maintaining tradition and adapting to change. While Confucianism values the preservation of moral and cultural traditions, it also recognizes the need to respond to the evolving needs of society. The principle of **Zhong Yong** (the Doctrine of the Mean) provides guidance in navigating this tension, advocating for a balanced approach that honors tradition while embracing innovation where necessary. This balance ensures that reforms are grounded in ethical principles but flexible enough to address contemporary challenges.

Another challenge lies in addressing systemic inequalities that can perpetuate social disharmony. While Confucianism upholds a hierarchical vision of society, it also emphasizes the ruler's duty to promote the welfare of all citizens, particularly the most vulnerable. The concept of **Minben**, or "the people as the foundation," underscores this responsibility. Confucius taught that a ruler's legitimacy depends on their ability to ensure the well-being of their people. Social reform, therefore, must prioritize policies and practices that reduce poverty, protect rights, and create opportunities for all individuals to thrive.

In the modern era, Confucian principles of social reform offer valuable insights for addressing global challenges. Issues such as economic inequality, environmental degradation, and political corruption disrupt harmony on a societal scale, demanding ethical and sustainable solutions. The Confucian emphasis on collective responsibility and moral leadership provides a framework for tackling these issues, encouraging leaders and citizens alike to act with integrity and prioritize the common good.

For instance, the Confucian ideal of harmony with nature has particular relevance in the context of environmental reform. Confucianism teaches that humanity is an integral part of the natural order, and that living in harmony with the environment is essential for societal well-being. This perspective calls for sustainable practices that respect ecological balance and ensure the long-term health of the planet. Similarly, the Confucian focus on community and solidarity can inform efforts to address social fragmentation, fostering a sense of shared purpose and mutual support in the face of global challenges.

At its heart, Confucian social reform is a holistic process that integrates moral, cultural, and institutional dimensions. It recognizes that true reform cannot be achieved through coercion or superficial changes but requires a deep and enduring commitment to ethical principles. By fostering virtue at every level—from the individual to the state—Confucianism envisions a society where justice, compassion, and harmony prevail.

This vision of social reform is both timeless and timely. It reminds us that the pursuit of a just and harmonious society is an ongoing endeavor, requiring constant reflection, adaptation, and effort. As Confucius observed, "The journey of a thousand miles begins with a single step." By taking that step—whether through personal growth, family engagement, or civic action—we contribute to the larger project of reforming society and bringing it closer to the ideal of harmony.

Chapter 41
Practical Rituals

Rituals in Confucianism, known as **Li**, are much more than mere formalities or expressions of devotion. They are the living fabric that binds individuals to their community, their ancestors, and the cosmos itself. By enacting rituals, Confucianism teaches, we align ourselves with the moral and spiritual order of the universe, achieving harmony on personal, familial, and societal levels. Yet, these rituals are not confined to grand ceremonies—they permeate the daily lives of individuals, offering a means to cultivate virtue, structure relationships, and reinforce shared values.

Confucius regarded **Li** as essential to human life, comparing its absence to a society without order or a home without foundation. The rituals he described are steeped in both tradition and symbolism, drawing upon ancient practices yet imbued with ethical purpose. Far from rigid or mechanical, they demand sincerity and understanding from those who perform them. As Confucius himself said, "The essence of ritual lies not in the formalities but in the respect and reverence they cultivate."

The role of rituals begins within the family. Central to Confucian thought is the veneration of ancestors—a practice that exemplifies gratitude and respect for one's origins. Ancestral rites, often performed during specific festivals or family gatherings, serve to honor past generations while fostering a sense of continuity and belonging. These rituals typically involve offerings of food and incense, prayers, and the recitation of family histories. Each gesture underscores the Confucian belief that individuals exist not in isolation but as part of an unbroken lineage, with responsibilities to both their forebears and descendants.

Beyond the family, rituals extend to the broader community, manifesting in rites of passage, public ceremonies, and cultural festivals. Confucianism views these communal rituals as opportunities to strengthen social bonds and affirm shared values. In traditional Chinese villages, for instance, rituals marking the harvest season would unite farmers, officials, and scholars in a spirit of gratitude and cooperation. Such ceremonies often involve music, dance, and offerings to **Tian**, or Heaven, emphasizing humanity's interconnectedness with the natural and spiritual realms.

The Confucian commitment to ritual is not limited to the ceremonial sphere but finds expression in the rhythms of daily life. Even simple actions—sharing a meal, greeting a neighbor, or attending to one's attire—can be infused with the principles of **Li**. These seemingly mundane gestures carry profound ethical significance, as they reflect the individual's respect for others and commitment to propriety. For example, the act of bowing in traditional Chinese culture, governed by Confucian etiquette, demonstrates humility and recognition of another's dignity.

Such rituals also serve a regulatory function, guiding behavior and resolving potential conflicts. In the workplace, rituals of deference—such as addressing superiors with honorific titles—ensure a harmonious environment where respect for hierarchy fosters cooperation. In education, the Confucian emphasis on rituals shapes the teacher-student relationship, instilling discipline and mutual respect through structured interactions. In governance, rituals reinforce the moral authority of leaders, who are expected to embody the virtues they espouse through public acts of integrity and benevolence.

One of the most enduring rituals in Confucian tradition is the formal practice of self-cultivation. This ritual, while inwardly focused, is no less profound in its implications for society. It involves daily reflection on one's actions, recitation of classical texts, and adherence to ethical principles in all endeavors. For

Confucius, such introspection was the cornerstone of personal growth and a prerequisite for meaningful participation in society. "To govern oneself," he taught, "is to govern the world."

Rituals also provide a bridge between the individual and the cosmos, aligning human actions with the rhythms of nature and the moral order of Heaven. The Confucian reverence for **Tian** is evident in rituals that mark the changing seasons or celestial events, such as the Winter Solstice Festival. These observances underscore humanity's dependence on natural cycles and the importance of living in harmony with them. Offerings made to Heaven during such rituals are not acts of petition but expressions of gratitude and acknowledgment of the interconnectedness of all life.

Modernity has, in many ways, eroded the traditional practice of rituals, leading some to question their relevance in contemporary life. Yet, Confucianism offers a compelling argument for their revival, emphasizing their adaptability and enduring value. In a world characterized by rapid change and social fragmentation, rituals provide stability and a sense of belonging. They remind individuals of their shared humanity and ethical obligations, offering a counterbalance to the isolating forces of technology and consumerism.

Consider, for example, how Confucian principles of ritual could be integrated into modern workplace cultures. Rituals of acknowledgment—such as regular expressions of gratitude between colleagues or the observance of milestones—can foster mutual respect and a sense of community. Similarly, rituals of mindfulness, adapted from Confucian self-cultivation practices, can help individuals navigate the pressures of contemporary life with clarity and purpose.

In the realm of education, the Confucian emphasis on ritual provides a framework for cultivating character alongside intellect. Classroom rituals that encourage students to reflect on their actions, respect their peers, and engage with classical texts can create an environment that nurtures ethical and intellectual growth. In governance, public rituals of accountability—such as leaders making transparent commitments to their constituents—can restore trust and moral integrity to political institutions.

Despite their evolving forms, rituals remain vital to the Confucian vision of a harmonious society. They are not relics of the past but dynamic practices that adapt to the needs of the present while preserving the wisdom of tradition. As Confucius observed, "Rituals are the thread that weaves the fabric of civilization."

By engaging in rituals, individuals connect not only with their immediate surroundings but also with the deeper currents of human history and the universal order. These practices remind us that every action, no matter how small, contributes to the greater harmony of the world. Through rituals, Confucianism invites us to transcend the mundane and rediscover the sacred in our daily lives.

In contemplating the role of rituals, we are reminded that they are both a reflection and a catalyst of virtue. They shape the character of individuals, the cohesion of families, and the moral fabric of societies. As we navigate the complexities of modern life, the Confucian wisdom of **Li** offers a timeless guide, urging us to cultivate respect, reverence, and harmony in all that we do.

Chapter 42
Daily Conduct

Confucianism's teachings reach into the most ordinary aspects of life, offering a vision of daily conduct as a profound expression of virtue and harmony. For Confucius, the true test of moral character was not found in extraordinary acts of heroism but in the quiet discipline of daily behavior. Every action, no matter how small, was an opportunity to cultivate virtue and demonstrate respect for the interconnected fabric of human relationships.

At the heart of Confucian daily conduct lies the principle of **Ren**, or humanity. This virtue permeates even the simplest gestures, guiding interactions with kindness, empathy, and sincerity. It is expressed in acts such as helping a neighbor carry their burden, speaking words of encouragement to a struggling friend, or taking a moment to listen to the concerns of others. For Confucius, these actions were not optional; they were essential practices that reinforced the bonds of community and cultivated a life of moral integrity.

Equally central to daily conduct is **Li**, the framework of propriety and etiquette that ensures interactions are conducted with respect and order. While Li is often associated with grand rituals, its relevance extends to everyday exchanges. Greeting someone with a bow, offering a seat to an elder, or maintaining a respectful tone during conversation are examples of Li in action. These practices, simple as they may seem, serve as constant reminders of one's responsibilities to others and the importance of maintaining harmony in all relationships.

Consider the Confucian emphasis on the family as a model for daily conduct. In a household guided by Confucian principles, every interaction reflects a commitment to mutual respect and care. Parents express their love for their children not only through affection but also through their dedication to teaching virtues and setting a moral example. Children, in turn, demonstrate their filial piety through acts of obedience, gratitude, and attentiveness. Even mundane activities—sharing a meal, performing household chores, or discussing the day's events—become opportunities to reinforce these values and deepen familial bonds.

In the workplace, Confucian daily conduct emphasizes diligence, integrity, and cooperation. A Confucian approach to professional life is rooted in the idea that work is not merely a means of earning a livelihood but a chance to contribute to the greater good. Employees are encouraged to approach their tasks with sincerity and attention to detail, while employers are expected to lead by example, treating their staff with fairness and compassion. Through consistent practice of these principles, the workplace becomes a microcosm of Confucian harmony, where individual efforts align with collective goals.

Daily conduct also extends to one's relationship with the self. For Confucius, self-discipline was a cornerstone of moral development. He believed that individuals should regularly examine their thoughts and actions, asking themselves if they have lived up to the virtues they espouse. This practice of self-reflection, known as **Shen**, fosters self-awareness and accountability, enabling individuals to identify areas for improvement and remain steadfast in their pursuit of virtue. Confucius himself exemplified this practice, famously stating, "Each day, I examine myself on three matters: whether I have been faithful in my duties, sincere in my dealings, and diligent in my studies."

Confucian daily conduct also finds expression in the rhythms of public life. In community settings, individuals are encouraged to act as role models, upholding values of generosity and fairness in their interactions. Simple acts such as assisting someone in need, resolving disputes peacefully, or showing gratitude for the contributions of others reflect the Confucian ideal of contributing to the collective well-being. These behaviors not only strengthen community ties but also inspire others to emulate virtuous conduct, creating a ripple effect of harmony and goodwill.

In education, the Confucian approach to daily conduct emphasizes respect for teachers, attentiveness in learning, and humility in the pursuit of knowledge. Students are taught to view education as a moral endeavor rather than a mere accumulation of facts. Simple habits such as arriving on time, preparing for lessons, and participating respectfully in discussions embody the Confucian belief that discipline in small matters lays the foundation for success in larger pursuits.

Confucius also recognized the role of environment in shaping daily conduct. He advised individuals to surround themselves with virtuous companions and avoid influences that might lead them astray. "The gentleman associates with those who help him cultivate virtue," he observed, "while the petty person seeks companions who encourage his faults." This teaching underscores the idea that one's daily choices—whether in friendships, activities, or habits—have a profound impact on moral character and overall well-being.

Even leisure activities are not exempt from the Confucian vision of daily conduct. Pastimes such as music, art, and calligraphy are celebrated in Confucianism for their capacity to refine the spirit and promote inner harmony. Engaging in these pursuits with sincerity and mindfulness transforms them into acts of self-cultivation. Similarly, time spent in nature—observing the changing seasons, tending to a garden, or walking through a quiet forest—provides opportunities for reflection and a renewed sense of connection to the natural order.

Critics may question whether such an all-encompassing vision of daily conduct is realistic or sustainable in the complexities of modern life. Confucianism responds by emphasizing adaptability and gradual progress. The teachings do not demand perfection but encourage individuals to strive for consistency and improvement. By integrating Confucian principles into small, manageable aspects of daily life, individuals can gradually cultivate habits that align with the broader ideals of harmony and virtue.

In the context of contemporary challenges, Confucian daily conduct offers timeless wisdom. In an age of digital distractions and fragmented relationships, the Confucian emphasis on attentiveness and sincerity reminds us to be fully present in our interactions. Amid growing polarization and conflict, the principles of respect and empathy provide a roadmap for bridging divides and fostering mutual understanding.

The beauty of Confucian daily conduct lies in its universality. Regardless of cultural or historical context, the teachings resonate with the fundamental human desire for meaningful relationships and a sense of purpose. By elevating everyday actions into expressions of virtue, Confucianism transforms the mundane into the profound, reminding us that every moment is an opportunity to cultivate harmony within ourselves and with the world around us.

In the words of Confucius, "The path of the gentleman begins with small steps." Through consistent practice of these small steps—acts of kindness, moments of reflection, gestures of respect—we move closer to realizing the Confucian vision of a life well-lived. Daily conduct, guided by these timeless principles, becomes not just a means of navigating the world but a path to inner and outer harmony, a testament to the enduring wisdom of Confucianism.

Chapter 43
Social Etiquette

Confucianism views etiquette as the invisible thread weaving the fabric of harmonious societies. While often overlooked in modern discourse, etiquette under Confucian thought transcends mere politeness. It is a deliberate practice rooted in **Li**—ritual propriety—that transforms social interactions into expressions of respect, integrity, and mutual understanding. In this light, social etiquette is both a reflection of personal virtue and a mechanism for cultivating collective harmony.

Confucian etiquette is deeply relational, emerging from the understanding that every human interaction carries the potential to affirm or disrupt harmony. Whether within the family, among friends, or in public settings, the observance of decorum reflects the individual's commitment to maintaining order and balance. For Confucius, how one acts toward others is inseparable from their moral character; social etiquette is thus a mirror of one's inner state.

One of the cornerstones of Confucian social etiquette is **deference**, the acknowledgment of another's dignity and role within the relational hierarchy. This principle is vividly embodied in familial settings, where children are taught to address their elders with humility and attentiveness. When a younger sibling waits patiently for an elder to speak, or when a child serves tea to their parent with both hands, these acts of etiquette communicate not only respect but also the enduring value of relationships.

This emphasis on deference extends to public interactions. Confucian teachings advocate for a composed demeanor, gentle speech, and a willingness to yield in contentious situations. In

Confucian thought, such behavior is not a sign of weakness but of strength, demonstrating one's mastery over impulsiveness and commitment to peace. For instance, yielding the right of way on a busy street or deferring to another's opinion in a non-critical debate may seem inconsequential, yet these actions build the foundations of mutual respect.

Central to Confucian social etiquette is the idea of **self-restraint**. Confucius taught, "Do not impose on others what you do not wish for yourself." This principle serves as a guiding light for interpersonal conduct, encouraging individuals to act with empathy and awareness. In practice, this could mean avoiding harsh criticism, respecting others' time, or refraining from actions that might cause discomfort. Self-restraint not only prevents discord but also fosters an environment where trust and goodwill can flourish.

Another dimension of social etiquette in Confucianism is **expressive moderation**. This entails balancing honesty with tact, ensuring that communication is both truthful and considerate. In Confucian thought, words hold great power; they can uplift and inspire or wound and alienate. Thus, the wise individual chooses their words carefully, avoiding unnecessary conflict while remaining true to their principles. Even in disagreement, Confucian etiquette emphasizes maintaining composure, addressing the issue rather than attacking the person, and seeking common ground.

In Confucian society, the concept of **ritualistic greetings** is a fundamental expression of etiquette. Bowing, exchanging pleasantries, or performing simple gestures of acknowledgment signify more than mere formalities; they affirm the presence and worth of others. Historically, these rituals were meticulously prescribed, reflecting the individual's status, role, and relationship to the person they greeted. Though modern societies may lack such rigid structures, the essence of these rituals persists in actions such as a firm handshake, a respectful nod, or a heartfelt thank you.

The practice of **gift-giving**, another element of Confucian social etiquette, exemplifies the balance between thoughtfulness and restraint. Gifts, in Confucian culture, are not evaluated by their material value but by the intention and appropriateness behind them. Offering a modest gift as a token of appreciation or remembrance strengthens bonds, while excessive or ostentatious giving can disrupt harmony by creating feelings of obligation or competition. Proper etiquette in giving lies in the ability to align the gesture with the occasion and the relationship it honors.

Confucian social etiquette also extends to larger societal interactions, particularly in maintaining **decorum during public events and gatherings**. Whether attending a banquet, a wedding, or a community meeting, individuals are expected to exhibit punctuality, attentiveness, and graciousness. Speaking out of turn, ignoring the needs of others, or drawing undue attention to oneself are seen as breaches of etiquette that disrupt the collective atmosphere. Conversely, observing these practices enhances the experience for all participants and reinforces the communal spirit.

The Confucian vision of etiquette further includes **environmental mindfulness**, reflecting the belief that respect extends beyond human relationships to encompass one's surroundings. In public spaces, this translates into behaviors such as keeping shared areas clean, conserving resources, and being mindful of noise levels. Such acts are not only practical but also expressions of gratitude for the shared world that sustains all life.

In the workplace, Confucian social etiquette emphasizes hierarchy, collaboration, and integrity. Employees are encouraged to respect the chain of command while leaders are reminded to act as moral exemplars. Courtesy in communication—whether addressing superiors, peers, or subordinates—creates an atmosphere of trust and cooperation. Small gestures, such as acknowledging a colleague's contributions or listening attentively during meetings, embody the Confucian ethic of respect.

Modern society often questions the relevance of formal etiquette, viewing it as restrictive or outdated. However, Confucianism offers a counterpoint, arguing that etiquette is not a superficial construct but a vital practice for cultivating meaningful relationships. Far from being rigid or prescriptive, Confucian etiquette adapts to context, guided by the timeless principles of respect, empathy, and balance.

In multicultural and globalized settings, Confucian social etiquette can serve as a bridge for understanding. The emphasis on humility, active listening, and reciprocity aligns with universal values, making these practices accessible across cultural boundaries. In moments of potential conflict—be it a cross-cultural business negotiation or a misunderstanding among diverse community members—the Confucian approach to etiquette provides tools for de-escalation and mutual appreciation.

The challenges of modern life, marked by digital communication and fast-paced interactions, present both obstacles and opportunities for practicing Confucian etiquette. Online platforms, for instance, often foster anonymity and impulsiveness, leading to misunderstandings or hostility. Applying Confucian principles in these contexts—through thoughtful messaging, respectful engagement, and avoidance of inflammatory language—can elevate the quality of digital discourse.

Ultimately, Confucian social etiquette is not an end in itself but a means to cultivate harmony and virtue. By practicing deference, self-restraint, and expressive moderation, individuals contribute to a society where respect and kindness prevail. As Confucius observed, "When one respects others, they will respect you; when one helps others, they will help you." This reciprocal dynamic is the essence of etiquette under Confucianism—a practice that, though rooted in the personal, reverberates across families, communities, and nations.

Through the lens of Confucianism, every interaction, no matter how brief, becomes an opportunity to uphold dignity, affirm connection, and reflect the shared humanity that binds us all. Social etiquette, far from being a mere convention, is revealed as a profound expression of the Confucian vision—a life lived in balance, respect, and harmony.

Chapter 44
Moral Practice

In Confucian philosophy, moral practice is not a static or abstract concept but an active, lived experience. It is the continuous application of ethical principles, such as **Ren** (benevolence) and **Yi** (justice), in one's daily actions and decisions. For Confucius, morality is not confined to theoretical discussions or grand gestures; instead, it is deeply embedded in the ordinary choices that define the rhythms of life. Moral practice transforms intention into action, shaping individuals and society in the pursuit of harmony and virtue.

The foundation of Confucian moral practice lies in **Ren**, the ultimate expression of humanity and empathy. Ren demands that individuals transcend self-interest and embrace a broader awareness of the needs and feelings of others. This virtue manifests in countless ways, from offering kindness to strangers to supporting family members in times of hardship. Yet, Ren is not simply a reaction to external circumstances—it is cultivated through reflection, discipline, and the persistent effort to align one's actions with ethical ideals.

Closely tied to Ren is the principle of **Yi**, which governs justice and righteousness. While Ren motivates actions from a place of compassion, Yi ensures that those actions are guided by fairness and integrity. In moral practice, Yi serves as a compass for making difficult choices, often requiring individuals to sacrifice personal gain for the greater good. For example, refusing to participate in corrupt practices, even at the cost of professional advancement, exemplifies how Yi operates as a moral anchor.

Central to the Confucian understanding of moral practice is the concept of **Li**, or ritual propriety. While often associated with formal ceremonies, Li extends to the small, structured habits that foster personal discipline and social harmony. By adhering to rituals—be it the respectful exchange of greetings, the observance of family traditions, or the mindful preparation of a meal—individuals cultivate a sense of order and intention in their lives. These rituals serve as reminders of one's moral commitments and provide a framework for consistent ethical behavior.

The Confucian ideal of moral practice also emphasizes **self-cultivation**. This process begins with introspection: a deliberate examination of one's thoughts, actions, and motivations. Confucius urged his disciples to ask themselves, "Have I been true in my interactions with others? Have I fulfilled my responsibilities today?" Such reflections are not meant to induce guilt but to inspire improvement. Self-cultivation is a dynamic journey, requiring humility to acknowledge flaws and resolve to correct them.

The practice of moral action is further enriched by the principle of **reciprocity**, encapsulated in the Golden Rule: "Do not impose on others what you do not wish for yourself." This timeless ethic challenges individuals to consider the impact of their actions on others, fostering relationships built on mutual respect and understanding. Reciprocity transforms morality from a solitary endeavor into a shared commitment, creating networks of trust and cooperation that benefit all members of society.

Confucianism recognizes that moral practice must adapt to context without compromising core principles. For instance, the demands of justice and benevolence may differ between family and public life. Within the family, where bonds of affection and loyalty are paramount, Ren might call for extraordinary acts of patience and forgiveness. In contrast, in governance or business, Yi might require impartiality and the enforcement of rules, even at the expense of personal relationships. This nuanced approach allows Confucian ethics to remain relevant across diverse spheres of life.

Historical examples offer profound insights into how Confucian moral practice operates in real-world scenarios. The story of Yan Hui, Confucius's favorite disciple, is particularly illustrative. Known for his humility and resilience, Yan Hui exemplified the virtues of Ren and Yi in his interactions with others. Despite facing poverty, he remained steadfast in his commitment to moral principles, choosing a life of simplicity and service over material wealth. His example underscores that moral practice is not measured by outward success but by the integrity of one's character.

At its core, moral practice in Confucianism is deeply relational. It acknowledges that individuals are not isolated entities but part of an intricate web of connections. This understanding places a profound responsibility on each person to act as a moral agent within their community. Whether by mediating disputes, mentoring younger generations, or volunteering for collective initiatives, Confucian moral practice encourages individuals to contribute actively to the well-being of others.

The principle of moral practice extends beyond interpersonal relationships to include one's **relationship with nature and the cosmos**. Confucius taught that harmony within society mirrors the broader harmony of the universe. Actions such as conserving natural resources, respecting the cycles of the seasons, and living in alignment with the rhythms of nature reflect a deep moral awareness. By honoring the interconnectedness of all life, individuals demonstrate their commitment to the Confucian ideal of balance and sustainability.

The challenges of modernity—marked by rapid technological advancements, economic pressures, and cultural shifts—pose unique obstacles to the consistent application of Confucian moral principles. For instance, in an era dominated by digital communication, maintaining authenticity and empathy in online interactions can be particularly challenging. Similarly, the pursuit of individual success often conflicts with the Confucian emphasis on collective welfare. Yet, these challenges also present opportunities to reaffirm and adapt moral practices in innovative ways.

In contemporary professional environments, for example, Confucian moral practice might manifest as ethical leadership. A manager inspired by Ren and Yi would prioritize the well-being of their team, fostering an inclusive and supportive workplace culture. Similarly, in education, teachers who embody Confucian values would not only impart knowledge but also serve as role models, nurturing their students' moral and intellectual growth. These applications demonstrate that Confucian moral principles remain a powerful guide for navigating complex modern contexts.

Another dimension of moral practice involves **nurturing moral courage**. Confucius recognized that acting ethically often requires standing firm against societal pressures or personal fears. This courage is not impulsive or reckless but rooted in a deep conviction of what is right. Examples include whistleblowers who expose corruption, activists who advocate for marginalized communities, or individuals who choose honesty over expediency in their personal relationships. Such actions, though difficult, reaffirm the transformative power of moral practice.

Ultimately, Confucian moral practice is a journey of transformation. It begins with the individual, whose disciplined efforts ripple outward, influencing families, communities, and societies. As Confucius himself observed, "To put the world in order, we must first put our nation in order; to put our nation in order, we must first put our family in order; to put our family in order, we must first cultivate our personal life." This cascading effect highlights the profound interconnectedness of moral practice and its potential to inspire collective change.

In a world often divided by conflict and self-interest, the Confucian emphasis on moral practice offers a beacon of hope. It challenges individuals to rise above short-term gains and align their actions with timeless principles of empathy, justice, and respect. Through deliberate and consistent practice, morality becomes more than an abstract ideal—it becomes a way of life that nurtures both personal fulfillment and societal harmony. In this way, Confucianism continues to illuminate the path toward a world where virtue reigns and humanity thrives.

Chapter 45
Spiritual Cultivation

In Confucian philosophy, the cultivation of the spirit represents a profound alignment between the self, society, and the cosmos. This aspect of Confucian practice transcends mere intellectual or moral development, inviting individuals to connect deeply with the universal principles that govern existence. While Confucianism is often perceived as pragmatic and socially oriented, its spiritual dimensions reveal an intricate tapestry of introspection, harmony, and reverence for the natural and metaphysical orders.

At the heart of spiritual cultivation is the concept of **Tian** (Heaven). For Confucius, Tian is not merely a divine entity but an embodiment of moral order and universal truth. Living in harmony with Tian requires individuals to attune themselves to its rhythms and principles, aligning their actions with a higher sense of purpose. This relationship is neither transactional nor fear-driven; it is a dynamic interplay of respect, gratitude, and an enduring commitment to uphold the moral laws embedded in the fabric of the cosmos.

The process of spiritual cultivation begins with **self-reflection**, a cornerstone of Confucian practice. Confucius emphasized the importance of examining one's thoughts and deeds, asking questions such as, "Am I fulfilling my moral duties? Have I acted with integrity today?" This introspection is not an act of self-reproach but a means of fostering self-awareness and clarity. Through reflection, individuals uncover their weaknesses and cultivate their strengths, moving closer to the ideal of moral and spiritual harmony.

A key element of spiritual cultivation is the practice of **rituals** (**Li**). While rituals are often associated with societal norms and ceremonies, they also serve as profound spiritual exercises. By participating in rituals with sincerity and mindfulness, individuals transcend their immediate concerns, connecting with the timeless traditions that unite humanity across generations. Whether honoring ancestors, observing seasonal changes, or engaging in everyday acts of courtesy, rituals anchor individuals in a larger spiritual framework, imbuing their actions with meaning.

Confucianism also emphasizes the cultivation of **inner tranquility**. This state of calm is not merely the absence of disturbance but an active balance of emotions, thoughts, and actions. Achieving inner tranquility requires the regulation of desires, the avoidance of excess, and the ability to find contentment in simplicity. Confucius believed that only a tranquil heart could perceive the true nature of Tian, likening this clarity to still water that reflects the heavens.

Meditation and **study** are integral to the spiritual path in Confucianism. Unlike the meditative practices of other traditions that may focus on detachment or transcendence, Confucian meditation centers on grounding oneself in ethical principles and reflecting on how to apply them in daily life. Similarly, the study of classic texts, such as the *Analects*, the *Great Learning*, and the *Book of Rites*, is not an academic pursuit but a spiritual exercise. These texts serve as guides, offering wisdom that inspires moral action and spiritual growth.

The cultivation of **compassion** further exemplifies the spiritual dimensions of Confucianism. Compassion is deeply rooted in **Ren** (benevolence), the supreme virtue that reflects humanity's potential for empathy and altruism. Spiritual growth involves expanding one's capacity for compassion, extending kindness not only to family and friends but also to strangers and even adversaries. This universal compassion mirrors the all-encompassing order of Tian, uniting the personal with the cosmic.

Confucian spiritual cultivation also incorporates a profound respect for **nature**. The cycles of the seasons, the flow of rivers, and the resilience of forests all embody the harmony and balance that Confucianism seeks to emulate. By observing and aligning with these natural rhythms, individuals gain insight into their place within the larger order. Planting crops in season, conserving resources, and showing gratitude for the earth's bounty are expressions of this spiritual connection.

In the realm of leadership, spiritual cultivation plays a critical role. A leader who has cultivated their spirit embodies the virtues of humility, wisdom, and moral clarity. Such a leader does not rule through coercion or fear but inspires through virtue and example, reflecting the harmony of Tian in their governance. The spiritual integrity of a leader, therefore, becomes a model for the entire community, fostering trust and unity.

Confucianism also recognizes the **communal aspect** of spiritual cultivation. While personal growth is essential, it is not pursued in isolation. Spiritual cultivation occurs within the context of relationships—family, friends, and society at large. The influence of a well-cultivated individual extends outward, inspiring others and creating a ripple effect of virtue and harmony. This interconnectedness reinforces the idea that spiritual development is both a personal and collective journey.

The challenges of modern life, with its rapid pace and material distractions, often obscure the path to spiritual cultivation. Yet, Confucian principles offer timeless guidance for navigating these complexities. For example, the practice of mindfulness in daily routines—whether through deliberate reflection, sincere interactions, or intentional rituals—provides a foundation for spiritual growth. Even in urban environments, moments of stillness and acts of kindness can reconnect individuals with the enduring values of Confucianism.

Historical figures exemplify the transformative power of spiritual cultivation. Take, for instance, Mencius, a prominent Confucian thinker whose spiritual depth and moral clarity inspired generations. Mencius emphasized the innate goodness of humanity, advocating for the cultivation of virtues that align with this inherent potential. His teachings remind us that spiritual cultivation is not about perfection but about nurturing the seeds of goodness within ourselves and others.

Spiritual cultivation in Confucianism also addresses the inevitability of suffering and impermanence. While Confucian philosophy does not focus explicitly on the afterlife, it provides a framework for finding meaning and purpose in the face of adversity. By aligning with Tian, cultivating virtue, and contributing to the well-being of others, individuals transcend their immediate circumstances, achieving a sense of fulfillment that outlasts physical existence.

The ultimate goal of spiritual cultivation is to achieve **harmony**—within oneself, with others, and with the universe. This harmony is not a static state but a dynamic equilibrium, requiring continuous effort and reflection. Confucius encapsulated this ideal in his assertion: "The superior person harmonizes but does not merely conform." This insight underscores the active and intentional nature of Confucian spirituality, where alignment with higher principles is achieved without losing one's individuality.

In a world increasingly fragmented by conflict and disconnection, the Confucian emphasis on spiritual cultivation offers a path toward unity and renewal. It challenges individuals to look beyond the surface, to seek depth in their actions and connections. By embracing the principles of Tian, Ren, and Li, and by committing to the lifelong journey of growth, individuals can find profound meaning and contribute to the flourishing of humanity.

Confucian spiritual cultivation, though deeply rooted in ancient traditions, remains a beacon for modern seekers. It reminds us that the spirit is not separate from the body or mind, but an integral part of our shared existence. Through deliberate practice, thoughtful reflection, and compassionate action, the cultivated spirit becomes a force for good—a living testament to the timeless wisdom of Confucianism.

Chapter 46
Personal Harmony

In the Confucian framework, personal harmony is not a passive state but an active pursuit—a balance between emotions, actions, and thoughts, rooted in self-awareness and ethical living. This harmony reflects the alignment of an individual's internal world with the external order of society and the cosmos, embodying the ideal of living in accordance with **Tian** (Heaven). It is a dynamic equilibrium, requiring constant reflection, discipline, and the cultivation of virtues.

At its core, personal harmony begins with the concept of **Zhong** (moderation). This principle emphasizes the avoidance of extremes and the pursuit of balance in all aspects of life. For Confucius, moderation was not a limitation but a guide to living well. It encouraged individuals to temper their desires, manage their ambitions, and maintain a sense of proportion in their interactions and responsibilities. By practicing moderation, one cultivates steadiness of character, essential for navigating the complexities of life.

The cultivation of personal harmony also relies heavily on the integration of **Li** (ritual propriety). Beyond its societal function, Li serves as a personal guide, structuring one's behavior and fostering discipline. By adhering to rituals—whether as simple as showing respect in conversation or as profound as observing ancestral rites—individuals connect their personal actions to a greater moral order. These rituals serve as a grounding force, enabling one to find stability amidst the unpredictability of daily life.

Another cornerstone of personal harmony is the mastery of **emotions**. While Confucianism does not advocate for the suppression of emotions, it emphasizes their regulation and appropriate expression. For instance, Confucius often spoke of the importance of **Ren** (benevolence) in relationships, which requires empathy and understanding. However, this empathy must be balanced with **Yi** (justice), ensuring that one's actions are guided by reason as well as compassion. By harmonizing emotions with ethical principles, individuals cultivate a temperament that is neither volatile nor detached but thoughtfully balanced.

Self-reflection, a recurring theme in Confucian thought, is an essential practice for achieving personal harmony. The process involves examining one's actions, thoughts, and intentions to ensure they align with moral and social ideals. Confucius himself exemplified this practice, stating, "Every day I examine myself on three points: In dealing with others, have I been unfaithful? In my interactions with friends, have I been insincere? Have I failed to practice what I preach?" This daily introspection fosters self-awareness and helps individuals identify areas where they may need to grow.

Central to the Confucian pursuit of personal harmony is the cultivation of **virtue**. Virtues such as Ren, Yi, and Xin (integrity) form the moral foundation of a harmonious life. However, Confucius viewed virtue not as an innate trait but as a quality that must be actively developed through education, practice, and reflection. By consistently striving to embody these virtues, individuals transform themselves, creating an internal balance that radiates outward to influence their relationships and communities.

The role of **knowledge** in personal harmony cannot be overstated. For Confucius, learning was a lifelong endeavor, a means of refining one's character and deepening one's understanding of the world. However, this knowledge was not meant to be purely theoretical; it had to be applied in service of moral improvement. Confucius taught that true wisdom lies in the ability to discern what is right and act accordingly. By integrating knowledge with virtue, individuals achieve a sense of purpose and coherence in their lives.

Confucianism also emphasizes the importance of relationships in cultivating personal harmony. The self, according to Confucius, does not exist in isolation but is deeply interconnected with others. Harmony in relationships—be it with family, friends, or society—reflects and reinforces internal harmony. The Five Cardinal Relationships (Wu Lun)—ruler and subject, father and son, husband and wife, elder and younger sibling, and friend and friend—serve as a framework for understanding how personal harmony is both shaped by and contributes to social harmony.

The principle of reciprocity, encapsulated in the Confucian maxim "Do not do to others what you do not wish for yourself," further guides interactions. By treating others with respect, fairness, and kindness, individuals create a positive cycle of mutual harmony. This reciprocal dynamic not only strengthens relationships but also reinforces one's own sense of balance and integrity.

In the context of modern life, achieving personal harmony presents unique challenges. The pace of contemporary society often leads to stress, distraction, and a disconnect from traditional values. However, Confucian principles offer practical tools for addressing these challenges. For instance, the practice of mindfulness—being fully present in one's actions and interactions—echoes Confucian teachings on attentiveness and sincerity. By cultivating awareness and intention in daily life, individuals can counteract the fragmentation and disorientation of modernity.

Personal harmony also involves cultivating resilience in the face of adversity. Confucius himself faced numerous setbacks, including political exile and professional failures, yet he remained steadfast in his principles. His life serves as a testament to the power of perseverance and moral clarity. By maintaining faith in one's values and continuing to strive for self-improvement, individuals can navigate difficulties without losing their sense of balance.

The cultivation of harmony extends to one's relationship with nature. Confucianism views humans as an integral part of the natural world, governed by the same rhythms and laws as the cosmos. Living in harmony with nature involves recognizing this interconnectedness and acting responsibly toward the environment. Simple practices, such as observing seasonal changes, conserving resources, and appreciating natural beauty, foster a sense of alignment with the larger order.

A life of personal harmony is also marked by the ability to find joy in simplicity. Confucius often spoke of the contentment that comes from a life well-lived, rooted in virtue rather than material wealth. He observed, "The noble person finds joy in virtue, while the small person finds joy in material gain." This perspective encourages individuals to focus on what truly matters: relationships, self-improvement, and contributing to the well-being of others.

The impact of personal harmony extends far beyond the individual. A harmonious person becomes a source of stability and inspiration for those around them. In families, they nurture love and respect; in communities, they promote trust and cooperation; in leadership, they exemplify integrity and fairness. This ripple effect illustrates the Confucian belief that personal harmony is the foundation of social and cosmic harmony.

Ultimately, the journey toward personal harmony is a lifelong process, requiring patience, discipline, and dedication. It is not a destination but a continual practice—a daily commitment to align one's inner self with the principles of Tian and the needs of society. Confucius encapsulated this ideal in his reflection: "At seventy, I could follow my heart's desires without transgressing what was right." This statement reveals the culmination of a life devoted to the pursuit of harmony: the seamless integration of personal freedom with moral responsibility.

Confucian teachings on personal harmony remain profoundly relevant today, offering a timeless blueprint for navigating the complexities of life. By embracing moderation, cultivating virtue, and fostering meaningful connections, individuals can create a sense of balance that sustains them in an ever-changing world. In doing so, they not only enrich their own lives but also contribute to the greater harmony of humanity and the cosmos.

Chapter 47
Individual Discipline

The essence of Confucian discipline lies in the deliberate cultivation of oneself—a commitment to excellence that transcends personal ambition and serves the greater harmony of society. Individual discipline, in this framework, is not a set of rigid rules but a way of life that aligns thought, action, and purpose with the principles of virtue and propriety. It is the foundation upon which personal character is built, relationships are nurtured, and societal harmony is sustained.

At its heart, discipline begins with **self-restraint**. Confucius taught that the first step toward self-improvement is the ability to regulate one's desires and impulses. This principle is encapsulated in the Confucian virtue of **Li** (ritual propriety), which governs not only public ceremonies but also personal behavior. By adhering to rituals and observing social norms, individuals develop the ability to act thoughtfully rather than react impulsively. This practice creates a foundation for measured, intentional action that reflects moral integrity.

Discipline in the Confucian sense also requires a profound commitment to **study and reflection**. Confucius himself was a lifelong learner, emphasizing that education is a process of continual growth. "To learn and to practice what is learned, is this not a great pleasure?" he remarked, linking the joy of learning with the discipline required to internalize and apply knowledge. Study, in this context, is not confined to academic pursuits but extends to self-examination and the cultivation of virtue. By reflecting on one's actions and refining one's understanding, discipline becomes a path to wisdom.

A critical component of individual discipline is the cultivation of **Ren** (benevolence) through daily practice. While Ren is often understood as the highest Confucian virtue, achieving it requires consistent effort and intentionality. Discipline is the mechanism through which one learns to act with empathy, compassion, and moral courage. This process involves small, deliberate actions—listening attentively, showing kindness, and acting with fairness—that collectively build a character rooted in Ren.

The Confucian emphasis on discipline extends to the management of time and priorities. The Analects contain numerous references to the value of diligence, such as, "The superior person is modest in speech but excels in action." This principle underscores the importance of focusing one's energy on meaningful endeavors, avoiding distractions, and resisting the temptation of superficial pursuits. Discipline in time management ensures that one's actions are purposeful and aligned with long-term goals, fostering both personal growth and societal contribution.

Integrity, or **Xin**, is another pillar of individual discipline. For Confucius, integrity meant consistency between one's words and actions, as well as a steadfast commitment to ethical principles. Discipline is required to maintain this alignment, especially in challenging circumstances. A disciplined person does not compromise their values for convenience or gain but remains true to their commitments. This consistency builds trust and strengthens relationships, making integrity both a personal and a communal virtue.

Discipline also manifests in the cultivation of **emotional balance**. Confucius recognized that emotions, while natural and essential, must be managed to prevent them from undermining one's judgment. He taught that anger, desire, and fear could disrupt harmony if left unchecked. Through discipline, individuals learn to moderate their emotions, expressing them in ways that are appropriate and constructive. This emotional regulation is not about suppression but about achieving a state of inner stability that allows for clear thinking and compassionate action.

In the realm of interpersonal relationships, discipline ensures that one adheres to the principles of reciprocity and respect. The Confucian ethic of **Do not impose on others what you do not wish for yourself** requires vigilance and self-control. It challenges individuals to act considerately, even when faced with provocation or disagreement. Discipline, in this sense, is a tool for maintaining harmony in relationships, fostering mutual understanding, and preventing conflict.

The practice of discipline extends to physical and mental well-being. Confucianism views the body and mind as interconnected, with each influencing the other. Therefore, caring for one's health is both a personal and a moral responsibility. Discipline in this area might involve regular exercise, a balanced diet, and mindfulness practices that enhance mental clarity and resilience. These habits not only benefit the individual but also enable them to fulfill their roles and responsibilities effectively.

For leaders, discipline takes on an additional dimension of accountability. Confucius emphasized that a ruler or leader must first cultivate themselves before seeking to govern others. "If you govern yourself, others will follow," he declared, highlighting the principle of leading by example. A disciplined leader inspires trust and loyalty, setting a standard for ethical behavior and diligent service. This approach creates a ripple effect, promoting discipline and virtue throughout the community.

The process of cultivating discipline often involves overcoming challenges and setbacks. Confucius himself faced numerous obstacles, yet he persisted in his quest for moral and intellectual growth. His perseverance serves as a model for those striving to develop discipline in their own lives. Each failure, when met with reflection and renewed effort, becomes an opportunity for growth. This resilience is a hallmark of Confucian discipline, transforming adversity into a catalyst for improvement.

Discipline is also closely tied to the concept of **Zhong** (loyalty), which in Confucianism refers to a sincere and wholehearted dedication to one's duties. Whether as a family member, friend, or citizen, discipline enables individuals to fulfill their roles with integrity and excellence. This sense of duty extends beyond personal relationships to include a commitment to the broader community. By practicing discipline in service to others, individuals contribute to the collective harmony envisioned by Confucius.

Modern life presents unique challenges to the cultivation of discipline, from the distractions of technology to the pressures of consumerism. However, Confucian teachings remain relevant, offering practical strategies for navigating these challenges. For instance, setting clear priorities, practicing mindfulness, and dedicating time to reflection can help individuals maintain focus and align their actions with their values. Discipline, in this context, becomes a means of resisting the fragmentation and superficiality of contemporary culture.

The rewards of individual discipline are profound and far-reaching. On a personal level, discipline fosters self-confidence, clarity of purpose, and a sense of fulfillment. It enables individuals to navigate life's complexities with grace and resilience. On a societal level, disciplined individuals serve as pillars of stability and integrity, inspiring others through their example and contributing to the collective good.

Ultimately, discipline is not an end in itself but a pathway to self-mastery and harmony. It is a dynamic process, requiring continual effort, reflection, and adjustment. Yet, as Confucius observed, the disciplined life is one of profound joy and meaning: "To see what is right and not do it is to lack courage." By choosing discipline, individuals align themselves with the highest ideals of humanity, transforming both their inner lives and the world around them.

Through discipline, the Confucian vision of a harmonious and virtuous society becomes attainable, one individual at a time. It is a practice that begins within but radiates outward, shaping families, communities, and nations. In this way, individual discipline is both a personal journey and a contribution to the enduring legacy of Confucian thought.

Chapter 48
Everyday Wisdom

Wisdom in Confucian thought is not confined to grand, abstract concepts or reserved for scholars and philosophers. It is rooted in the simplicity of daily life, in the ordinary moments that shape human experience. Everyday wisdom, or **Zhi**, represents the practical application of knowledge, morality, and insight to foster harmony and ethical living. This wisdom is not about knowing everything; rather, it is about understanding what is right, acting with virtue, and navigating life's complexities with grace and clarity.

Confucius saw wisdom as a guiding light in human behavior, a quality that bridges the gap between thought and action. He taught that wisdom begins with **understanding oneself**. To truly know oneself—one's strengths, weaknesses, motivations, and values—is the foundation of wise living. This self-awareness allows individuals to align their actions with their principles, creating a life of integrity and purpose. It also fosters humility, as one recognizes the limits of their knowledge and remains open to learning from others.

A key component of everyday wisdom is **discernment**—the ability to distinguish between right and wrong, essential and trivial, beneficial and harmful. In Confucian ethics, this discernment is guided by the principles of **Yi** (justice) and **Ren** (benevolence). A wise person considers not only their own needs but also the impact of their actions on others. They weigh their decisions carefully, seeking a balance that upholds fairness and promotes the well-being of all involved.

In practice, wisdom often reveals itself in small, seemingly mundane decisions. Consider a parent teaching a child the value of respect, a worker handling a conflict with patience, or a friend offering honest advice. Each of these actions, when guided by virtue and thoughtfulness, embodies Confucian wisdom. It is through these ordinary acts that the seeds of harmony are sown, creating ripple effects that extend to families, communities, and beyond.

Confucius emphasized the importance of **learning from experience** as a pathway to wisdom. "He who learns but does not think is lost; he who thinks but does not learn is in danger," he said, underscoring the interplay between reflection and action. Wisdom is not static; it evolves as individuals encounter new challenges, adapt to changing circumstances, and grow from their successes and failures. Through reflection, one transforms experience into insight, making each day an opportunity for growth.

Another essential aspect of everyday wisdom is the ability to **listen and observe**. Confucius taught that wisdom comes not only from books and teachers but also from paying attention to the world around us. By observing the behavior of others, one can learn valuable lessons about virtue and vice, kindness and cruelty, diligence and laziness. Similarly, by listening—truly listening—to the thoughts and feelings of others, one gains a deeper understanding of human nature and strengthens their capacity for empathy.

Confucian wisdom also involves **embracing simplicity and balance**. In a world that often glorifies excess and complexity, the wise individual finds contentment in moderation. This principle is reflected in the Confucian ideal of **Zhongyong**, or the Doctrine of the Mean, which advocates for balance and harmony in all aspects of life. By avoiding extremes, whether in emotions, behavior, or material pursuits, one creates a stable foundation for happiness and fulfillment.

Adaptability is another hallmark of Confucian wisdom. Life is inherently unpredictable, filled with changes and uncertainties. A wise person does not resist these changes but adapts to them with resilience and creativity. This adaptability is not about compromising one's values but about finding new ways to uphold them in different circumstances. For example, in the face of adversity, a wise individual might turn a challenge into an opportunity for growth, demonstrating resourcefulness and inner strength.

In Confucianism, wisdom is deeply connected to **relationships**. The ability to maintain harmonious interactions with others is seen as a reflection of one's moral character and practical intelligence. Everyday wisdom guides individuals in navigating the complexities of human relationships, whether by resolving conflicts, showing gratitude, or offering support. It encourages sincerity, kindness, and respect, fostering connections that are both meaningful and enduring.

One of the most profound expressions of wisdom is the capacity for **compassionate leadership**. Confucius believed that those in positions of authority bear a special responsibility to act wisely, setting an example for others to follow. A leader guided by wisdom seeks not personal gain but the greater good, balancing firmness with kindness and decisiveness with humility. This principle applies not only to rulers and officials but to anyone who takes on a leadership role in their family, workplace, or community.

Confucian wisdom also teaches the importance of **patience and perseverance**. In a fast-paced world, the value of waiting, observing, and allowing time to unfold is often overlooked. Yet wisdom understands that some solutions require patience, that some lessons can only be learned over time. By cultivating perseverance, one develops the fortitude to endure difficulties and the clarity to make thoughtful decisions, even under pressure.

The practice of everyday wisdom is enriched by **gratitude and mindfulness**. Confucius encouraged his followers to appreciate the beauty of the present moment and to find joy in simple pleasures—sharing a meal with loved ones, witnessing the changing seasons, or engaging in meaningful work. Gratitude deepens one's connection to the world, fostering a sense of harmony and contentment that transcends material concerns.

For Confucius, the ultimate purpose of wisdom was to create harmony—not only within oneself but also in the broader social and natural order. He envisioned a world where individuals, guided by wisdom and virtue, worked together to build a just and peaceful society. This vision begins with the small, deliberate acts of wisdom practiced in daily life. By making wise choices in how they speak, act, and relate to others, individuals contribute to the greater harmony that Confucius saw as the highest ideal.

In the modern world, the principles of Confucian wisdom remain as relevant as ever. From managing the distractions of technology to addressing global challenges like inequality and climate change, the need for thoughtful, ethical decision-making is universal. Everyday wisdom provides a compass for navigating these complexities, offering timeless insights into how to live with integrity and purpose.

Ultimately, everyday wisdom is not an extraordinary gift but a skill that can be cultivated by anyone willing to learn, reflect, and grow. It is found in the quiet moments of self-discipline, the thoughtful interactions with others, and the mindful choices that shape our days. As Confucius himself said, "Wisdom is to know what is right; courage is to do it." By embracing this wisdom, individuals can create a life of meaning and contribute to a world of greater harmony.

In this way, everyday wisdom is both deeply personal and profoundly universal. It is the thread that weaves together the fabric of a virtuous life, guiding individuals to fulfill their potential and inspiring them to create a more just and compassionate society. Through the practice of wisdom in daily life, the teachings of Confucius come alive, offering a path to a better world—one thoughtful action at a time.

Chapter 49
Global Influence

The teachings of Confucianism, while rooted in ancient China, have radiated across continents, shaping cultures, governance, and ethical systems far beyond their place of origin. This enduring philosophy, with its emphasis on virtue, harmony, and social responsibility, has proven both adaptable and universal. The global influence of Confucian thought is not merely a relic of history but a living testament to its relevance across diverse contexts and epochs.

Confucianism first spread beyond China's borders during the Han Dynasty, when China's political and cultural influence extended to Korea, Japan, and Vietnam. Each of these regions embraced Confucian ideals, incorporating them into their unique cultural frameworks. In Korea, for example, Confucianism became the bedrock of the Joseon Dynasty's governance, with its focus on filial piety and hierarchical order aligning seamlessly with Korean values. Korean Confucian scholars contributed their interpretations to the tradition, creating schools of thought that enriched its legacy.

In Japan, Confucianism influenced both the samurai code of ethics and the governance of the Tokugawa Shogunate. The samurai's adherence to duty, loyalty, and self-discipline mirrored Confucian ideals of virtue and responsibility. Meanwhile, in Vietnam, Confucianism informed both education and governance, providing a moral framework for rulers and a scholarly foundation for civil service examinations. These adaptations demonstrate how Confucianism's core principles could be reinterpreted to address the specific needs of different societies.

As Confucianism spread, it did not remain static. Each culture that adopted its principles infused them with local traditions, creating a rich tapestry of interpretations. This adaptability is a hallmark of Confucian thought, which emphasizes practical wisdom and ethical flexibility. By prioritizing values such as respect, justice, and communal harmony, Confucianism provided a universal language for addressing the complexities of human relationships and governance.

The global influence of Confucianism extends beyond East Asia. During the 16th century, Jesuit missionaries brought Confucian texts to Europe, translating works such as the *Analects* and the *Doctrine of the Mean* into Latin. European philosophers, including Voltaire and Leibniz, were deeply impressed by Confucianism's ethical clarity and its emphasis on moral education. They saw it as a rational and humanistic tradition that offered an alternative to dogmatic religious systems.

Voltaire, in particular, praised Confucius as a "great philosopher" who governed through virtue rather than coercion. He admired the Confucian ideal of leadership, where rulers lead by example, earning the respect of their subjects through moral integrity. For Enlightenment thinkers, Confucianism represented a model of governance that harmonized reason and morality, inspiring debates about ethics, politics, and the role of education in society.

In the modern era, Confucianism continues to shape global discussions about ethics, governance, and cultural identity. Its emphasis on respect for tradition and communal responsibility has influenced debates on sustainable development, social justice, and intergenerational equity. For instance, the Confucian concept of **Ren** (benevolence) resonates with contemporary calls for global solidarity and compassion, while its focus on **Li** (ritual) underscores the importance of cultural preservation in a rapidly changing world.

Confucian values have also played a significant role in the economic rise of East Asia. The so-called "Confucian work ethic," which emphasizes diligence, discipline, and education, has been credited with driving the rapid industrialization and modernization of countries like South Korea, Japan, and Singapore. This ethic, rooted in the Confucian ideal of self-cultivation, encourages individuals to strive for excellence while contributing to the collective good.

At the same time, the resurgence of Confucianism in China reflects its enduring relevance in navigating modern challenges. As China grapples with the complexities of globalization, Confucianism offers a framework for balancing tradition and progress. The revival of Confucian education, including the establishment of Confucius Institutes worldwide, underscores the importance of this philosophy in promoting cultural exchange and understanding.

However, the global influence of Confucianism has not been without challenges. Critics have argued that Confucian ideals, particularly their emphasis on hierarchy and obedience, can perpetuate authoritarianism and social inequality. Others have questioned its relevance in societies that prioritize individual rights over collective responsibilities. These critiques highlight the need for a nuanced understanding of Confucianism, recognizing both its strengths and its limitations.

Despite these challenges, Confucianism's ability to inspire dialogue and adaptation underscores its vitality. In multicultural and pluralistic societies, its emphasis on mutual respect and harmony provides a valuable framework for fostering understanding and cooperation. The Confucian ideal of **He** (harmony), which seeks balance and reconciliation among diverse perspectives, aligns with global efforts to address conflicts and build inclusive communities.

Confucianism also offers a counterbalance to the hyper-individualism of contemporary culture. Its focus on relationships—between family members, citizens, and the natural world—encourages a sense of interconnectedness and shared responsibility. This perspective is particularly relevant in addressing global challenges such as climate change, where collective action and long-term thinking are essential.

In education, Confucian principles continue to shape teaching and learning practices worldwide. The emphasis on lifelong learning, moral development, and respect for teachers resonates with educational philosophies across cultures. The Confucian ideal of **Zhi** (wisdom) reminds educators and students alike that true knowledge is not merely about acquiring information but about cultivating character and applying insights for the greater good.

The influence of Confucianism is also evident in contemporary discussions of leadership. The Confucian model of governance, which prioritizes ethical leadership and accountability, offers a powerful counterpoint to models that prioritize power or profit over people. In business, politics, and community organizations, the Confucian ideal of leading by example serves as a reminder that true authority is earned through integrity and service.

As the world becomes increasingly interconnected, the teachings of Confucianism offer a bridge between cultures and traditions. Its emphasis on dialogue, empathy, and ethical reflection fosters mutual respect and shared understanding, creating opportunities for collaboration and innovation. By addressing universal human concerns, Confucianism transcends its historical and geographical origins, offering timeless wisdom for navigating the complexities of modern life.

In reflecting on the global influence of Confucianism, one is reminded of the profound adaptability of its principles. Whether in ancient courts or contemporary classrooms, Confucianism continues to inspire individuals and societies to strive for virtue, harmony, and wisdom. It reminds us that the pursuit of ethical living is not confined to any one culture or era but is a shared endeavor that unites humanity in its quest for a just and compassionate world.

Through its enduring legacy, Confucianism demonstrates the power of ideas to transcend boundaries, bridging the past and the present, the East and the West. It challenges us to consider what it means to live well, to lead with virtue, and to contribute to the flourishing of all. In this way, the teachings of Confucius remain not only relevant but essential, guiding humanity toward a future defined by understanding, cooperation, and shared purpose.

Chapter 50
Modernity and Confucianism

In the whirlwind of modernity, where technology evolves at an unprecedented pace and societies wrestle with global challenges, Confucianism emerges as both a historical touchstone and a contemporary guide. Its principles, rooted in the ancient past, confront the realities of an interconnected world, offering solutions that transcend time. As humanity navigates the complexities of inequality, environmental crises, and social fragmentation, the philosophy of Confucius continues to assert its relevance with profound clarity.

The modern era, defined by its focus on individualism, rapid economic development, and the global exchange of ideas, presents unique challenges to Confucian ideals. However, rather than being displaced, Confucianism has shown remarkable resilience, adapting to these shifts while maintaining its core values of harmony, virtue, and collective responsibility. This duality of tradition and innovation lies at the heart of Confucianism's modern resurgence.

One of the most compelling aspects of Confucian thought in the 21st century is its potential to address the social and ethical voids left by globalization and modernization. The Confucian emphasis on **Ren** (humanity) and **Li** (ritual) provides a counterbalance to the alienation and transactional relationships that often characterize contemporary life. In a world increasingly dominated by digital interactions, Confucianism reminds us of the importance of genuine human connection, empathy, and shared purpose.

The revival of Confucianism in modern China exemplifies this adaptability. Over the past few decades, the Chinese government has embraced Confucian principles to shape policies and promote cultural identity. This revival is evident in the establishment of Confucius Institutes worldwide, which aim to foster cultural exchange and introduce the world to Chinese language and philosophy. By reclaiming its Confucian heritage, China seeks not only to honor its past but also to navigate the future with a moral compass rooted in its own traditions.

Yet, this resurgence has not been without controversy. Critics argue that the state's use of Confucianism risks reducing its profound teachings to mere political tools. The tension between Confucian ideals of virtue and the realities of statecraft raises important questions about how philosophical traditions can coexist with contemporary governance. Nevertheless, the revival underscores the enduring relevance of Confucianism in shaping national identity and moral discourse.

Beyond China, Confucian principles have found resonance in addressing global issues such as environmental sustainability. The Confucian concept of **Tian** (Heaven) emphasizes humanity's interconnectedness with nature, promoting a vision of harmony between people and the environment. This perspective aligns with modern ecological movements, which advocate for stewardship, balance, and the recognition of our shared responsibility to future generations.

For instance, Confucianism's advocacy for moderation and respect for natural resources offers a philosophical foundation for sustainable development. The idea of **He** (harmony) underscores the need for balance—not only between humanity and nature but also within economic and social systems. By integrating these principles into contemporary environmental policies, societies can draw upon ancient wisdom to create innovative solutions for pressing challenges.

In the realm of social justice, Confucianism addresses issues of inequality through its emphasis on moral leadership and the equitable distribution of resources. The Confucian ideal of **Yi** (justice) insists on fairness and integrity, urging leaders to prioritize the common good over personal gain. This principle resonates with modern calls for ethical governance and corporate responsibility, encouraging decision-makers to act with accountability and compassion.

Education, another cornerstone of Confucianism, remains a critical area where its teachings can inspire progress. The Confucian model of lifelong learning and moral cultivation offers a framework for holistic education in the modern world. As societies grapple with the challenges of misinformation, social polarization, and a rapidly changing job market, Confucianism's emphasis on critical thinking, ethical reflection, and the integration of knowledge and virtue provides a powerful antidote.

The Confucian commitment to **Xin** (trustworthiness) also offers valuable lessons for building integrity in modern institutions. In an era marked by political corruption and corporate scandals, the Confucian ideal of trust underscores the importance of honesty, consistency, and accountability in fostering strong relationships and effective governance. By prioritizing trust, organizations can cultivate cultures of transparency and collaboration, reinforcing social cohesion and public confidence.

However, the modern relevance of Confucianism is not without its challenges. The philosophy's emphasis on hierarchy and familial roles, for instance, has been criticized as incompatible with contemporary values of equality and individual rights. Feminist scholars, in particular, have questioned the gendered aspects of Confucian traditions, arguing for reinterpretations that uphold its core ethical principles while embracing modern commitments to inclusivity.

Despite these critiques, Confucianism's capacity for reinterpretation has enabled it to remain relevant across diverse contexts. By focusing on its foundational principles—virtue, harmony, and communal responsibility—Confucianism continues to offer insights that transcend cultural and temporal boundaries.

Its flexibility allows it to evolve in response to contemporary challenges while retaining its philosophical essence.

One of the most striking examples of Confucianism's modern application is its potential to foster intercultural dialogue. In a world marked by division and misunderstanding, Confucianism's emphasis on mutual respect and ethical reciprocity provides a framework for bridging differences. The Confucian concept of **Shu** (empathy) reminds us to consider the perspectives of others, fostering a spirit of cooperation and understanding that is essential for navigating global conflicts.

In the corporate world, Confucian principles have influenced approaches to leadership and organizational culture. The Confucian ideal of leading by example emphasizes the importance of moral integrity and humility, encouraging leaders to inspire trust and loyalty through their actions. This approach aligns with modern theories of servant leadership, which prioritize the well-being of employees and stakeholders over hierarchical authority.

As technology reshapes human experience, Confucianism offers a grounding ethical perspective. The rise of artificial intelligence, for example, raises profound questions about morality, agency, and the future of work. Confucian ethics, with its focus on humanity and relational responsibility, can guide the development of technologies that enhance rather than diminish human dignity. By embedding Confucian values into the design and deployment of technology, societies can ensure that innovation serves the greater good.

In family and community life, Confucianism continues to inspire practices that nurture connection and resilience. The emphasis on filial piety, for instance, encourages intergenerational solidarity and mutual care. In an age where social bonds are often weakened by mobility and individualism, Confucian values provide a counterbalance, reminding us of the importance of shared responsibility and the strength of communal ties.

Ultimately, the modern relevance of Confucianism lies in its ability to address universal human concerns while adapting to diverse cultural and historical contexts. It challenges us to consider what it means to live ethically in a complex and interconnected world, offering timeless principles that guide us toward harmony, wisdom, and collective flourishing.

As societies continue to evolve, Confucianism's teachings remain a vital resource for navigating the moral and practical dilemmas of modernity. Its enduring emphasis on virtue, respect, and responsibility serves as a beacon, reminding us of our shared humanity and our capacity to build a just and compassionate world. In this way, Confucianism bridges the ancient and the modern, illuminating a path forward that honors the past while embracing the possibilities of the future.

Chapter 51
Cultural Dialogue

In the intricate web of human civilization, where cultures, religions, and philosophies collide and intertwine, Confucianism stands as a profound voice advocating mutual understanding and harmony. As a philosophy deeply rooted in respect for relationships and the pursuit of ethical living, it provides a lens through which diverse traditions can engage in meaningful dialogue. In an era defined by globalization and interdependence, the wisdom of Confucianism offers a compelling framework for fostering empathy, collaboration, and a shared vision of human dignity.

At the heart of Confucianism lies the principle of **Shu**—often translated as reciprocity or empathy—which urges individuals to "not impose on others what you would not want for yourself." This foundational idea transcends cultural and linguistic boundaries, resonating with ethical teachings found in many world traditions. In the context of cultural dialogue, **Shu** encourages a willingness to listen, to understand, and to find common ground, even amidst differences. It is a call for humility and openness, virtues that are indispensable in bridging divides and building meaningful connections.

Confucianism's emphasis on **Li** (ritual propriety) also offers insights into the mechanisms of respectful interaction. While **Li** often refers to ceremonial practices, its broader interpretation includes norms of behavior that uphold respect and order in social interactions. In intercultural exchanges, the concept of **Li** reminds us of the importance of acknowledging and honoring the customs and values of others. It underscores the idea that understanding another's worldview begins with respect for their traditions and practices.

Historically, Confucianism has played a pivotal role in shaping the cultural and philosophical dialogue across East Asia. Its principles influenced the development of societies in Korea, Japan, and Vietnam, where Confucian ethics were adapted to local contexts, creating unique cultural syntheses. This cross-pollination exemplifies the adaptability of Confucianism and its capacity to enrich and be enriched by diverse traditions.

For instance, in Korea, Confucianism merged with indigenous values and Buddhist thought, creating a framework that emphasized filial piety, education, and communal harmony. In Japan, it integrated with Shinto and Zen Buddhism, contributing to the cultivation of discipline, respect, and hierarchical order. In Vietnam, Confucian ideals became foundational to governance and social organization, shaping the values of duty and moral integrity. These adaptations highlight how Confucianism has historically fostered dialogue, allowing cultures to find resonance and synergy within its teachings.

In the modern era, Confucianism continues to inspire intercultural collaboration. The establishment of Confucius Institutes around the world exemplifies its role in promoting cultural exchange and education. These institutes serve as platforms for introducing Confucian philosophy and Chinese culture to global audiences, encouraging mutual understanding and appreciation. However, they also raise questions about the balance between cultural education and political influence, reminding us of the complexities inherent in cultural diplomacy.

The Confucian ideal of **Ren** (humanity or benevolence) is particularly relevant in addressing the challenges of global dialogue. **Ren** calls for compassion and a deep sense of responsibility toward others, emphasizing the interconnectedness of all human beings. In a world often marked by division and mistrust, **Ren** provides a moral compass for navigating differences with grace and integrity. It encourages us to approach cultural dialogue not as a contest of ideologies, but as a shared journey toward understanding and collective well-being.

Confucianism's compatibility with other philosophical and religious traditions further enhances its potential as a bridge in cultural dialogue. Its principles align with similar values found in other systems of thought, such as the Buddhist emphasis on compassion, the Christian ideal of love thy neighbor, and the Islamic principle of mutual respect. These intersections create opportunities for meaningful engagement and shared exploration of ethical and spiritual questions.

For example, interfaith dialogues often highlight the shared ethical foundations between Confucianism and other traditions. Discussions on topics such as the role of virtue, the importance of family, and the pursuit of social harmony reveal profound commonalities, fostering mutual respect and cooperation. Such dialogues not only deepen understanding but also create avenues for collaborative action in addressing global issues such as poverty, climate change, and conflict resolution.

Confucianism's approach to leadership also offers insights into the dynamics of cultural dialogue. The Confucian ideal of the **Junzi**—the noble person—emphasizes self-cultivation, moral integrity, and leading by example. In the context of intercultural interactions, this ideal encourages participants to embody the virtues they advocate, fostering trust and credibility. A true leader in cultural dialogue is one who listens, learns, and acts with humility and fairness, qualities that are deeply rooted in Confucian teachings.

However, Confucianism is not without its challenges in the modern discourse on cultural dialogue. Critics argue that its traditional emphasis on hierarchy and deference to authority may conflict with contemporary values of equality and individual rights. These tensions highlight the need for critical reinterpretation, ensuring that Confucian principles are applied in ways that honor both tradition and modern ethical standards.

One area where Confucianism has demonstrated remarkable adaptability is in its engagement with contemporary movements advocating for gender equality. While traditional Confucian texts often reflect patriarchal norms, modern reinterpretations have sought to highlight the gender-neutral aspects of its ethical teachings, such as the universality of **Ren** and the shared responsibility for moral cultivation. These reinterpretations open the door for Confucianism to contribute to dialogues on gender equity and social justice.

In the realm of diplomacy, Confucian principles provide a framework for constructive engagement between nations. The emphasis on mutual respect, reciprocity, and harmony aligns with the goals of international cooperation and conflict resolution. For example, the Confucian focus on dialogue and consensus-building resonates with the practices of mediation and peacebuilding, offering insights into how nations can navigate complex negotiations with integrity and fairness.

The Confucian concept of **He** (harmony) further underscores the importance of balance in cultural dialogue. **He** is not about uniformity or erasing differences but about finding equilibrium and creating a space where diverse perspectives can coexist and enrich one another. This vision of harmony is particularly relevant in multicultural societies, where fostering inclusivity and cohesion requires acknowledging and valuing diversity.

Ultimately, Confucianism challenges us to approach cultural dialogue with a sense of shared humanity and moral responsibility. It calls for an ethic of care, reminding us that our interactions with others are not merely transactions but opportunities to build meaningful relationships. Whether in personal exchanges, community interactions, or global forums, Confucian principles provide a timeless guide for navigating the complexities of cultural engagement.

As the world becomes increasingly interconnected, the need for thoughtful and compassionate dialogue grows ever more urgent. Confucianism, with its rich ethical tradition and emphasis on relational harmony, offers a profound resource for meeting this need. By embracing its teachings, we can cultivate a spirit of empathy, respect, and collaboration, paving the way for a more harmonious and interconnected world.

Chapter 52
Contemporary Challenges

Confucianism, with its millennia of history and rich philosophical tradition, stands as a beacon of moral guidance and social harmony. Yet, the modern world presents challenges that test the adaptability and relevance of its teachings. In an era marked by rapid technological advancement, urbanization, globalization, and individualism, Confucian principles must navigate a complex landscape while retaining their foundational values. How does a philosophy rooted in ancient China address the realities of the 21st century?

One of the most pressing challenges is the tension between traditional Confucian hierarchies and contemporary values of equality and human rights. Confucianism places great emphasis on social roles and hierarchies, as seen in the **Wu Lun** (Five Cardinal Relationships): ruler and subject, parent and child, husband and wife, elder and younger sibling, and friend and friend. These relationships, while fostering order and respect, often assume inherent power dynamics, particularly in the roles of ruler, parent, and husband.

In modern contexts, these hierarchical structures can conflict with ideals of gender equality, individual autonomy, and democratic governance. For example, the traditional Confucian view of filial piety (**Xiao**) as absolute obedience to parents may clash with contemporary notions of mutual respect and personal freedom within families. Similarly, the emphasis on deference to authority raises questions about the compatibility of Confucianism with participatory democracy and the protection of individual rights.

To address these tensions, contemporary scholars and practitioners have sought to reinterpret Confucian principles in ways that align with modern values. Rather than viewing hierarchy as rigid and oppressive, they emphasize its potential to foster mutual care and responsibility. In this view, the roles of parent, ruler, and elder are reimagined not as positions of domination but as responsibilities to nurture, guide, and protect. Such reinterpretations allow Confucianism to retain its ethical core while evolving to meet the demands of modern society.

Another significant challenge is the rise of individualism, a defining characteristic of modernity that often stands in stark contrast to Confucianism's emphasis on community and collective well-being. Confucian ethics prioritize relationships and the fulfillment of social roles, viewing the individual as inseparably connected to the family, community, and state. However, in contemporary urbanized and globalized societies, where personal achievement and self-expression are often celebrated, the collective focus of Confucianism can feel restrictive.

This shift toward individualism is particularly evident among younger generations, who may prioritize career ambitions, personal happiness, and global mobility over traditional family obligations. The Confucian ideal of **Ren** (humaneness), which emphasizes empathy and selflessness, must now contend with questions about how to balance individual desires with responsibilities to others. Can Confucianism offer a framework for integrating personal freedom with communal harmony?

The answer may lie in its concept of **Zhong Yong** (the Doctrine of the Mean), which advocates balance and moderation. Rather than rejecting individualism outright, Confucianism can encourage individuals to pursue personal growth and fulfillment in ways that also contribute to the well-being of their communities. For example, a young professional seeking career success might also support their parents financially or mentor younger colleagues, embodying the Confucian ideal of harmony between personal and collective goals.

Globalization presents another complex challenge for Confucianism. As cultures and economies become increasingly interconnected, traditional philosophies must engage with diverse worldviews and navigate the influence of global ideologies. For Confucianism, this means addressing both opportunities and criticisms that arise from its interaction with Western thought, particularly liberalism and capitalism.

Liberalism, with its focus on individual rights and freedoms, often critiques Confucianism's emphasis on duty and hierarchy as overly constraining. Meanwhile, the capitalist ethos of competition and profit-seeking may appear at odds with Confucian values of humility, integrity, and communal care. These critiques, while valid, also provide opportunities for Confucianism to adapt and contribute to global discourse.

For instance, Confucian ethics can offer a counterbalance to the excesses of capitalism, advocating for sustainable practices and ethical business leadership. The concept of **Yi** (righteousness) emphasizes moral integrity over personal gain, encouraging leaders to prioritize long-term social benefits over short-term profits. Similarly, Confucian ideas about reciprocity and mutual care can inform global efforts to address economic inequality and environmental degradation, promoting a vision of shared responsibility and interdependence.

Urbanization, another hallmark of modernity, also poses challenges to Confucianism's traditional focus on family and rural life. The rapid growth of cities often leads to fragmented communities, weakened family ties, and a sense of anonymity that contrasts sharply with Confucian ideals of close-knit relationships and communal support. In urban settings, how can Confucian values of filial piety, neighborly respect, and social harmony be preserved?

One possible answer lies in the Confucian concept of **Li** (ritual propriety), which emphasizes the importance of structure and intentionality in human interactions. In an urban context, this could translate into creating spaces and practices that foster connection and community, such as neighborhood initiatives, mentorship programs, and public rituals that celebrate shared values. By adapting traditional practices to urban environments, Confucianism can help bridge the gap between modern lifestyles and its ethical teachings.

Technological advancement, particularly in artificial intelligence and digital communication, presents another frontier for Confucian thought. The rise of AI raises profound ethical questions about the nature of relationships, responsibility, and humanity itself. How should Confucianism address the role of technology in shaping human interactions and decision-making?

Confucian principles offer valuable insights into these questions. The emphasis on relational ethics, for example, can guide the development of AI systems that prioritize empathy, fairness, and accountability. Similarly, the Confucian focus on self-cultivation and lifelong learning can encourage individuals to use technology not as a substitute for human effort but as a tool for personal and social growth.

At the same time, digital communication and social media challenge Confucian ideals of face-to-face interaction and deep relational bonds. The Confucian emphasis on sincerity and respect in relationships must be reimagined for a world where interactions often occur through screens and algorithms. This reimagining requires a careful balance, preserving the depth of traditional relationships while embracing the possibilities of digital connectivity.

The environmental crisis represents yet another urgent challenge that Confucianism is uniquely positioned to address. Its emphasis on harmony with nature, rooted in the concept of **Tian** (Heaven or the natural order), aligns with contemporary calls for ecological sustainability. Confucianism views humanity as part of a larger cosmic order, with a responsibility to care for the environment as stewards of the natural world.

In addressing climate change, Confucian values of moderation and intergenerational responsibility can inspire collective action. For example, the Confucian principle of **Cheng** (sincerity) emphasizes the need for genuine commitment to ethical behavior, encouraging individuals and governments to adopt sustainable practices with integrity and consistency.

Ultimately, the adaptability of Confucianism lies in its ability to reinterpret its teachings in light of new challenges without losing its ethical foundation. By embracing dialogue, critical reflection, and creative application, Confucianism can remain a vital force in addressing the complexities of the modern world.

As societies grapple with questions of identity, justice, and sustainability, Confucianism's timeless wisdom offers a moral compass for navigating change. Its emphasis on harmony, reciprocity, and self-cultivation reminds us that the challenges of today, though formidable, can be met with principles that honor both tradition and innovation. In doing so, Confucianism continues to illuminate a path toward a more ethical and harmonious future.

Chapter 53
Eternal Legacy

As the final chapter unfolds, the legacy of Confucianism reveals itself not merely as a relic of ancient thought, but as a living tradition that continues to inspire, challenge, and guide humanity. Its enduring relevance lies in the universality of its core principles—virtue, harmony, and the relentless pursuit of moral excellence. Across the centuries, Confucianism has shaped societies, enriched cultures, and provided a philosophical framework for individuals seeking a life of purpose and balance.

The story of Confucianism's eternal legacy begins with its profound influence on the civilizations of East Asia. From the Han Dynasty's formal adoption of Confucian principles to Japan's Tokugawa shogunate and Korea's Joseon Dynasty, Confucianism became the bedrock of governance, education, and social conduct. The structures of meritocratic bureaucracy, the veneration of scholarship, and the moral foundations of leadership were all deeply infused with Confucian ideals.

Even as dynasties fell and new ideologies emerged, Confucianism adapted. During the Tang and Song dynasties, the fusion of Confucianism with Buddhist and Daoist thought gave rise to Neo-Confucianism, a renaissance of philosophical inquiry and ethical refinement. Figures like Zhu Xi and Wang Yangming reinvigorated Confucian teachings, exploring the metaphysical and psychological dimensions of self-cultivation. Their contributions ensured that Confucianism would not stagnate but evolve, deepening its relevance in changing contexts.

The legacy of Confucianism is not confined to the annals of history or the borders of East Asia. In modern times, its principles have found resonance in global discourses on ethics, education, and governance. The Confucian concept of **Ren** (humaneness) parallels universal ideals of compassion and altruism, while **Yi** (justice) and **Li** (propriety) align with contemporary notions of fairness and social cohesion.

Educational systems worldwide continue to draw inspiration from Confucian emphasis on lifelong learning and the moral development of character. The practice of cultivating wisdom through reflection, dialogue, and disciplined study reflects Confucianism's timeless commitment to self-improvement and intellectual growth. Institutions that uphold values of academic excellence, ethical leadership, and civic responsibility unknowingly echo the Confucian ideal of harmonious balance between personal achievement and societal contribution.

Confucianism's political legacy is equally profound. At its heart lies the conviction that governance must be rooted in virtue and the welfare of the people. This principle challenges leaders across all cultures and systems to prioritize moral integrity over power, to lead by example, and to foster trust through ethical conduct. While the world has witnessed periods when Confucian ideals were misinterpreted or used to justify authoritarianism, the essence of Confucian political thought remains a call for justice, accountability, and the cultivation of virtuous leadership.

In the context of globalization, Confucianism emerges as a bridge between cultures. Its emphasis on mutual respect and dialogue offers a model for fostering understanding in an increasingly interconnected world. As nations grapple with the complexities of cultural diversity, Confucian principles of harmony and reciprocity provide a philosophical foundation for peaceful coexistence.

Environmental stewardship, a pressing concern of the 21st century, also finds a powerful ally in Confucianism. The philosophy's reverence for **Tian** (Heaven) and its call to live in harmony with the natural world resonate deeply in the age of climate change and ecological crisis. Confucianism urges humanity to act as responsible stewards of the earth, recognizing that our actions today shape the inheritance of future generations.

Yet, the true measure of Confucianism's eternal legacy lies not in its historical achievements or global influence, but in its capacity to transform individuals. The Confucian path is one of **self-cultivation**, a lifelong journey of becoming a better person through reflection, learning, and virtuous action. This journey begins within but radiates outward, touching families, communities, and societies.

Confucius's teachings remind us that greatness is not reserved for the extraordinary but is achieved through the ordinary acts of kindness, integrity, and perseverance. A person who embodies **Ren** uplifts others, a leader guided by **Yi** inspires trust, and a community grounded in **Li** flourishes in harmony. In this way, Confucianism transcends the boundaries of time and place, offering wisdom that is as relevant to a scholar in ancient Lu as to a citizen of the modern world.

Critics have argued that Confucianism's focus on tradition and hierarchy makes it ill-suited for contemporary times. Yet, its enduring legacy lies precisely in its adaptability. Confucianism does not demand blind adherence to the past but invites thoughtful engagement with its principles. Each generation has the opportunity to reinterpret its teachings, preserving its essence while addressing the unique challenges of its era.

This adaptability is evident in the revival of Confucian thought in modern China and beyond. As societies seek ethical frameworks to navigate the complexities of modernization, Confucianism offers guidance rooted in compassion, wisdom, and responsibility. Its emphasis on education, ethical leadership, and community resonates with universal aspirations for a just and harmonious world.

The story of Confucianism is far from complete. Its legacy continues to unfold, carried forward by those who see in its teachings a path to a more ethical and meaningful existence. Scholars and practitioners, educators and leaders, families and individuals—all contribute to the living tradition of Confucianism, ensuring that its wisdom endures.

As the final lines of this journey are written, the words of Confucius echo across the ages: *"To learn and to practice what is learned time and again, is this not a pleasure? To have friends coming from afar, is this not a joy? To be unperturbed when not understood by others, is this not the mark of a noble person?"*

These simple yet profound reflections encapsulate the heart of Confucianism: the joy of learning, the value of relationships, and the strength of character. They remind us that the legacy of Confucianism is not merely an inheritance from the past but a call to action for the present and future.

The path of Confucius invites each of us to cultivate virtue, to build harmonious relationships, and to contribute to the greater good. In embracing this path, we not only honor a timeless tradition but also shape a legacy of our own—one that inspires future generations to walk with integrity, wisdom, and compassion.

And so, the legacy of Confucianism endures, as eternal as the principles it espouses and as vibrant as the lives it touches. It is not merely a philosophy but a way of being, an invitation to seek harmony within ourselves, with others, and with the world. In this pursuit, Confucianism lives on, a testament to the timeless power of virtue, wisdom, and humanity.

Epilogue

As this journey through the *Rituals of Unity* comes to a close, a profound understanding unfolds: harmony is not a static state but a delicate dance between tradition and transformation, the individual and the collective, the human and the cosmic. This book has not merely sought to present a philosophy or retell the story of a tumultuous era; it has aimed to guide you toward a reunion with yourself, with the essence that connects the intimate to the universal.

The lessons of Confucianism echo in every gesture, every choice, every relationship that shapes life. *Ren*, humanity, reminds us that true strength lies in compassion. *Yi*, justice, challenges us to act with integrity, even when it requires sacrifice. *Li*, the rituals, show us that the sincere repetition of virtuous actions can transform chaos into order, both within ourselves and in the world around us.

As you close this book, you are not ending a reading experience; you are beginning a new chapter of your existence. What aspects of your life are calling for greater alignment with virtue? What interactions could be elevated through a more conscious practice of humanity? These questions have no definitive answers but open doors to reflections that will continue to guide you far beyond this moment.

The work that now concludes is an invitation to continuity. Every page you have read is not merely a memory; it is a seed planted. The teachings of Confucius and the sages who followed him are not static monuments but rivers that flow, adapting to the terrain of each era and each reader. Allow these waters to transform your inner soil, nourishing new ideas, actions, and connections.

You entered this book seeking knowledge. Now you leave with something more valuable: the possibility of integrating this wisdom into your life, shaping not only your choices but also the world around you. The learning here does not end; it reverberates, expanding in circles that touch the infinite. May you walk with courage and clarity, always remembering that harmony is not a destination but the path itself.

www.ingramcontent.com/pod-product-compliance
Lightning Source LLC
LaVergne TN
LVHW040047080526
838202LV00045B/3528